Ace Your SHRM Certification Exam
Third Edition

ACE YOUR SHRM CERTIFICATION EXAM

THIRD EDITION

The *Official* SHRM Study Guide for the SHRM-CP® and SHRM-SCP® Exams

Plus 50 SHRM-CP/SHRM-SCP Practice Items

Editors: Charles Glover, MS, Manager, Exam Development & Accreditation, SHRM and Nancy A. Woolever, MAIS, SHRM-SCP, Vice President, Academic, Certification and Student Communities

Society for Human Resource Management
Alexandria, Virginia shrm.org

Society for Human Resource Management India
Mumbai, India shrm.org/in

Society for Human Resource Management
Middle East and Africa Office
Dubai, UAE shrm.org/mena

This publication is designed to provide accurate and authoritative information regarding the subject matter covered. It is sold with the understanding that neither the publisher nor the author is engaged in rendering legal or other professional service. If legal advice or other expert assistance is required, the services of a competent, licensed professional should be sought. The federal and state laws discussed in this book are subject to frequent revision and interpretation by amendments or judicial revisions that may significantly affect employer or employee rights and obligations. Readers are encouraged to seek legal counsel regarding specific policies and practices in their organizations.

This book is published by SHRM, the Society for Human Resource Management. The interpretations, conclusions, and recommendations in this book are those of the author and do not necessarily represent those of the publisher.

SHRM is a member-driven catalyst for creating better workplaces where people and businesses thrive together. As the trusted authority on all things work, SHRM is the foremost expert, researcher, advocate, and thought leader on issues and innovations impacting today's evolving workplaces. With nearly 340,000 members in 180 countries, SHRM touches the lives of more than 362 million workers and their families globally. Discover more at SHRM.org.

Library of Congress Cataloging-in-Publication Data

Names: Glover, Charles (Manager at SHRM), editor.
Title: Ace your SHRM certification exam : the official SHRM study guide for the SHRM-CP and SHRM-SCP exams / editor, Charles Glover, M.S., Manager, Exam Development & Accreditation, SHRM.
Description: Third edition. | Alexandria, Virginia : Society for Human Resource Management, [2024] | "Plus 50 SHRM-CP/SHRM-SCP Practice Items" | Includes bibliographical references and index. | Summary: "The third edition of this short, accessible guide to demystify the SHRM-CP and SHRM-SCP certification exams includes additional practice questions along with expert tips for understanding, studying, practicing, and acing the tests"-- Provided by publisher.
Identifiers: LCCN 2024026471 (print) | LCCN 2024026472 (ebook) | ISBN 9781586446918 (trade paperback) | ISBN 9781586446963 (pdf) | ISBN 9781586447052 (epub) | ISBN 9781586447106 (kindle edition)
Subjects: LCSH: Personnel management--Examinations--Study guides. | Personnel management--Examinations, questions, etc. | Personnel departments--Employees--Certification.
Classification: LCC HF5549.15 .A34 2024 (print) | LCC HF5549.15 (ebook) | DDC 658.30076--dc23/eng/20240614

All product names, logos, and brands are property of their respective owners in the United States and/or other countries. All company, product, and service names used on this website are for identification purposes only. SHRM®, SHRM-CP®, SHRM-SCP®, Learning System®, SHRM BASK™, and the "SHRM" logo are registered trademarks of SHRM.

Published in the United States of America

THIRD EDITION   2025 REVISED PRINTING

PB Printing   10 9 8 7 6 5 4 3 2   SHRMStore SKU: 61.14523

Contents

PART 4
Exam Day

APPENDIXES

Foreword

Congratulations! We are glad you are here to continue your journey with SHRM by pursuing SHRM certification. By reading and using this book, we hope that you walk away feeling confident and prepared for your upcoming SHRM certification exam. In this book, you will gain deeper insights into the SHRM-CP® and SHRM-SCP® certification exams backed by insights curated through SHRM research, examinee feedback, HR professionals' stories, and self-reflection culminating in the suggestions and advice reflected here. All these pieces of advice are presented to you here because they ultimately lead to higher percentages of certificants succeeding on either exam.

Creating this book, along with the SHRM-CP and SHRM-SCP workbooks that accompany it, the editors strive to demystify not only the SHRM exams, but the SHRM BASK® in a way that delves deeper into SHRM's multiple preparation tools and study aids and provides key information that can be found in no other products on the market. Whether you just started your HR career, or you are at a senior HR career level, you are in the right place to kick-start your SHRM certification journey, which is an achievement in and of itself.

SHRM hopes you will embrace certification as a critical step in a lifelong commitment to knowing, doing, learning, and growing as an HR professional. Your commitment to your own growth and development helps you create a better workplace and a better world. In this book, we provide tools to guide you on your journey toward success on the SHRM-CP or SHRM-SCP certification exam. We recommend you leverage these resources to succeed. This study guide

» Provides an easy-to-use roadmap to help understand the design and development of the SHRM exams and exam items therein with expert tips—for understanding the SHRM-developed materials, studying best practices, practicing with prior SHRM test items, and managing pretest anxiety so you can perform at your best on exam day;

» Covers everything you need to know about the exams, including exam construction, subject matter expert-developed content, exam structure in relation to the SHRM BASK, eligibility requirements, exam administration, in person versus remote proctoring, scoring, results, other SHRM learning resources, and more;

» Features interviews with experts and tips from real test takers on preparing for the exam and reducing test anxiety;

» Shows how to create a study plan based on your individual learning style and proven strategies for effective studying;

» Highlights how to practice taking the exam and how to best use the included 50-question practice-item sets;

» Includes ready-to-use tools, templates, and worksheets to guide study and practice plans; and

» Supplies detailed learning and study resources, including a summary of the terms and acronyms commonly used on the exam.

We also include special features that help you focus, organize, and plan your study time before taking the exam. These include

» Quotes, stories, and advice from former test takers;

» Key point summaries, infographics, and additional information highlighted for quick reference;

» Activities, including self-assessments and reflection tools; and

» Examples to illustrate core concepts.

Obtaining SHRM certification is a huge achievement, but your journey is only just beginning. The field of HR is an ever-changing landscape that we all must adapt to and influence to continue serving our partners, stakeholders, and organizations. With that comes additional learning and opportunity to gain further mastery of HR knowledge and refine your skillset to use what you know to behave competently in the workplace as an HR leader. Once you earn the SHRM-CP or SHRM-SCP credential, recertifying every three years becomes the next critical step toward your continued learning, growth, and competence as an HR professional—and SHRM will continue to work with you as your life-long HR career partner.

Our hope is to prepare you to take either the SHRM-CP or SHRM-SCP exam so you feel confident that you have given yourself the best possible chance of passing. If you would like additional access to prior SHRM-CP or SHRM-SCP exam items for practice, check out the SHRM-CP Workbook or SHRM-SCP Workbook—each serves as a deeper dive into the SHRM BASK, and each has seventy additional practice items.

We look forward to becoming and remaining a trusted partner in your career journey and we welcome the opportunity to support you as you learn, grow, know, and contribute to your workplace, develop as a professional, and advance the HR profession through those contributions. With SHRM certification awaiting you on the next step on your journey, we wish you success on the exam.

Best of luck, and happy studying!

—Michael P. Aitken, executive vice president,
HR Professional Solutions,
Society for Human Resource Management,
Alexandria, Virginia

Introduction

Twenty years from now you will be more disappointed by the things that you didn't do than by the ones you did do. So, throw off the bowlines, sail away from safe harbor, catch the trade winds in your sails. Explore, Dream, Discover.

—Mark Twain

The SHRM-CP® and SHRM-SCP® are the first-ever behavioral competency-based certifications for HR generalists, setting a new global standard in certification for the HR profession. By achieving and maintaining SHRM certification, you are making a commitment to lifelong learning about human resources.

HR professionals increasingly use the term *competency* to describe a complex set of interrelated skills, knowledge, and abilities that are often associated with success in a specific job. This reflects the fact that acquiring specific knowledge is not always enough to produce the desired performance of certain tasks. Competencies—measurable or observable knowledge, skills, abilities, and other characteristics critical to successful job performance—fill this gap. Competency frameworks provide further structure around those competencies needed for job success.

SHRM set a goal of raising the caliber of the human resources profession. To do this, SHRM realized that the profession had to apply the principles of competencies and competency frameworks to its occupation. HR needed to identify what competencies were associated with effective, high-performing HR professionals. SHRM conducted this research with HR professionals in 33 countries. More than 32,000 HR professionals participated in the development and validation of the eventual competency model which, since its inception, has been reviewed and validated by separate panels of global HR experts regularly to reflect the continuously evolving nature that is global HR. SHRM's competency model reflects the breadth of HR's successful practice with various constituents, which includes

» The entire organization vertically, from senior management to new hires;

» All divisions and functions of the organization horizontally; and

» External stakeholders as well as internal customers.

To succeed in this broad role, an HR professional must possess and demonstrate the nine competencies described in the SHRM Body of Applied Skills and Knowledge® (SHRM BASK):

Leadership	Interpersonal	Business
Leadership & Navigation	Relationship Management	Business Acumen
Ethical Practice	Communication	Consultation
Inclusion & Diversity	Global Mindset	Analytical Aptitude

HR Expertise, the technical competency, is the ability to apply HR principles and practices to the success of the organization. It is thoroughly defined in the fourteen functional areas of the SHRM BASK:

People	Organization	Workplace
HR Strategy	Structure of the HR Function	Managing a Global Workforce
Talent Acquisition	Organizational Effectiveness & Development	Risk Management
Employee Engagement & Retention	Workforce Management	Corporate Social Responsibility
Learning & Development	Employee & Labor Relations	U.S. Employment Law & Regulations
Total Rewards	Technology Management	

Why Take the Certification Exam?

Each year, we survey thousands of former test takers to learn what role certification plays in their career development. These certified HR professionals say that it enhances their credibility, helps them compete in the job market, increases their confidence, and keeps them up to date on developments in the HR field.

SHRM-certified professionals also

» Focus on continuously improving themselves and their organizations;

» Earn more, are more employable, and are more likely to receive promotions;

» Possess more relevant skill sets, demonstrate more leadership potential, and are more productive; and

» Feel more satisfied with their careers and benefit from the support of a professional community.

Why This Book?

We wrote this book to share what we've learned from successful test takers about what worked when they prepared for and took a SHRM certification exam, including

» Their insights on what it was like to prepare for a challenging exam,

» What they discovered about how their HR experience helped them succeed,

» How they created and stuck to a workable study plan and schedule so they would be ready on test day,

» How they managed any feelings of nervousness or anxiety they experienced,

» What test-taking strategies they used to help them answer the exam questions, and

» How studying the SHRM Learning System® in conjunction with the SHRM BASK yields the highest pass rate percentages compared to any other preparation tool for both the SHRM-CP and SHRM-SCP exams.

Additionally, we identified informational gaps that SHRM is eager to fill, ensuring that all test takers have the necessary information at their disposal to make informed decisions regarding SHRM-developed test preparation products providing relevant, accessible, affordable, and powerful tools to support your goal of becoming SHRM certified to create better workplaces for a better world.

How the Book Is Organized

In Part 1, you'll find an overview of SHRM certification and the SHRM-CP and SHRM-SCP exams; an overview of the SHRM BASK; guidance for determining which exam you are eligible to take; and an explanation of how the exams are created, administered, and scored.

Part 2 includes an exploration of learning styles so you can discover how you learn best. It also contains proven strategies for studying effectively and guidance for creating a study plan that makes the most of your study time.

Part 3 covers the best practices for successful test taking. It will show you how to draw on your HR experience and what you learn from studying to answer the questions on the exam, as well as strategies for reducing test anxiety and procrastination.

Part 4 gives you a preview of what to expect on test day, including information about taking the exam in a Prometric test center or via remote proctoring. It also covers what happens after you take an exam.

The appendices contain helpful documents to support your learning journey, including 50 practice questions and answer keys composed of 25 SHRM-CP and 25 SHRM-SCP exam questions for practice, a glossary of terms, an acronym list used on the SHRM certification exams, and much more.

How to Use This Book

There are a variety of ways to prepare for the SHRM certification exams. It is recommended that you couple this study guide with SHRM's other offerings as prior exam feedback and pass rate data indicate the highest chances of success.

You can study on your own, using this book as a guide. However, a more comprehensive preparation tool may suit your needs beyond what this book offers. Our research shows that using additional methods of preparation increases your chance of passing. Using this book as your guide, SHRM offers a variety of other preparation products to meet your needs including

» The SHRM BASK, a free resource that doubles as the content blueprint for both exams;

» The SHRM Learning System, the comprehensive certification preparation resource (which is available via flexible self-study and instructor-led options, as well as team-learning options for organizations—and through partner universities that are authorized to teach the SHRM Learning System content);

» A variety of webinars are available in the SHRM Store; and

» You can join with other certification candidates to form a study group, many of which form organically through SHRM chapters.

SHRM also offers additional study aids containing deeper insights into the exams including preparation insights and SHRM-developed SHRM-CP and SHRM-SCP practice questions, each having appeared on an actual SHRM test. This and more can be found in this and two other study aids: the *SHRM-CP Workbook* and the SHRM-SCP Workbook.

Whichever method or methods you choose, a key part of your preparation will be thinking through the types of situations, challenges, problems, and opportunities you encounter in your day-to-day HR work. This study guide is designed to supplement the preparation methods that are the best fit for you.

How This Book Was Developed

This book is a collaborative effort among the SHRM staff in various divisions along with expert assistance from a seasoned book writer and editor and SHRM-certified subject matter experts. There are many moving parts in test development and administration, so each internal expert contributed their piece of the puzzle to provide you with a complete picture of the exam, the test-day experience, and what it takes to prepare. Our goal is to provide as much helpful information in one source as possible and to dispel myths about the SHRM certification exams so that you can be ready for success on test day.

The first edition of this book was published in 2019. To reflect the ever-changing nature of the exam, SHRM revised and expanded the book in 2022, and again in 2024 with this third edition. A few of the major changes include the following:

» Updated content to further reflect the changes in the 2022 SHRM BASK.

» Deeper insights into the SHRM BASK and how it should be used when preparing for either the SHRM-CP or SHRM-SCP exams.

» Additional information about remote testing and how to decide whether this option is the best one for you.

» Revised information about the structure of the exam, including the total testing time and number of exam questions.

» New chapter about the most and least effective strategies for reasoning through an item, with examples (see Chapter 9).

» Increased number of questions in the practice test section (see Appendix 2).

A Word about What This Book Is NOT

This book is NOT intended to be a substitute for the SHRM BASK, nor the SHRM Learning System. For success on the SHRM certification exams, we encourage you to review the SHRM BASK carefully and use it to map out your study plan. Here's why:

» The SHRM BASK is a roadmap to every topic that is considered fair game for exam questions. It covers a wide variety of topics, and we suggest a focused review to augment and inform your study plan. Keep in mind that there are 134 questions on the exam compared with hundreds of key concepts and proficiency indicators presented in the SHRM BASK.

» The SHRM BASK represents the results from a comprehensive practice analysis—it is detailed and comprehensive because its contents represent the entirety of the practice of HR as validated through empirical research.

» As you review the SHRM BASK, use the content to differentiate between the areas you have mastered and those you need to learn more about. Identifying what you do and do not know about the topics covered in the SHRM BASK will help you craft a study plan and strategy that works best for you. We'll talk about this further in Part 2.

» Use the SHRM BASK as your launch point to map out your personal study plan. Everyone's path to certification is unique. SHRM offers an array of preparation products, from the SHRM Learning System to webinars, to the SHRM-CP and SHRM-SCP Workbooks, we have a tool to meet your needs.

Let's get started!

ONLINE

Access the interactive SHRM Body of Applied Skills and Knowledge (SHRM BASK) here:

https://www.shrm.org/credentials/certification/exam-preparation/bask

Acknowledgments

This resource was made possible by the thoughtful and generous advice, guidance, and input of many smart and talented subject matter experts, especially the following:

Mike Aitken, executive vice president, HR Professional Solutions, SHRM

Nicholas Schacht, SHRM-SCP, chief commercial officer, SHRM

Alexander Alonso, PhD, SHRM-SCP, chief data and insights officer, SHRM

Jeanne Morris, senior vice president, Consumer Products, SHRM

Patricia Byrd, SHRM-SCP, director, Credentialing Services, SHRM

Susie Davis, director, Education Products, SHRM

Hanna Evans, SHRM-CP, senior specialist, Form Development, SHRM

Eddice L. Douglas, SHRM-CP, lead, Educational Products, SHRM

Sarah Chuon, SHRM-CP, specialist, Exam Development, SHRM

Giselle Calliste, SHRM-CP, specialist, Exam HR Content, SHRM

Morgan Fecto, Exam Development, SHRM

Scott Oppler, PhD, senior technical advisor, Human Resource Research Organization (HumRRO)

Laura Steighner, PhD, president, Steighner Solutions

Kelly Cusick, senior vice president, Marketing, Holmes Corporation

Caitlin Shea, SHRM-CP, product manager, Holmes Corporation

Janis Fisher Chan, lead writer and developmental editor, first edition

We also gratefully acknowledge the scores of SHRM members, test takers, and exam candidates who volunteered to share their stories and offer tips for this book.

Part 1

About the SHRM-CP and SHRM-SCP Certification Exams

There are no limits. There are only plateaus, and you must not stay there—you must go beyond them.

—Bruce Lee

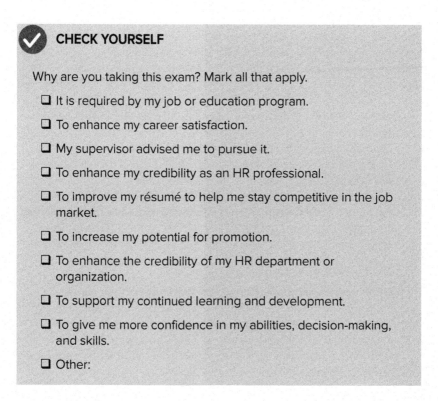

CHECK YOURSELF

Why are you taking this exam? Mark all that apply.

- ☐ It is required by my job or education program.
- ☐ To enhance my career satisfaction.
- ☐ My supervisor advised me to pursue it.
- ☐ To enhance my credibility as an HR professional.
- ☐ To improve my résumé to help me stay competitive in the job market.
- ☐ To increase my potential for promotion.
- ☐ To enhance the credibility of my HR department or organization.
- ☐ To support my continued learning and development.
- ☐ To give me more confidence in my abilities, decision-making, and skills.
- ☐ Other:

Identify Your Reasons for Pursuing Certification

Candidates who take the SHRM-CP and SHRM-SCP exams take them for many different reasons. It is important to think about why *you* are taking this exam because it will help you focus on achieving your goal to become SHRM-certified.

At some point during your certification study, your motivation will likely drop. You'll want to skip your study group, take a break from your flash cards for a few days, or give up on taking the exam altogether.

When that happens, revisit this page. Think about the specific reasons why you decided to start this journey and how you and your career will benefit from a SHRM credential. Then recommit to making it happen.

Career Benefits of SHRM Certification

Earning a SHRM-CP or SHRM-SCP certification has become increasingly valuable to HR professionals. Every HR professional who takes one of the exams has personal reasons for seeking certification, but the benefits of a SHRM certification are significant and widespread, as shown in a large study of HR professionals in 2020–2021.

» **Earning a SHRM certification credential can help you in your career growth.** Ninety-three percent of SHRM-certified HR professionals agreed that SHRM certification increases the likelihood of finding a comparable or better a job in the field of HR, and 88 percent agree it increases the likelihood of obtaining a promotion in the field of HR.

» **Obtaining a SHRM certification credential is related to higher salaries.** HR professionals who pass the SHRM-CP and SHRM-SCP certification exams report salaries that are 14 to 15 percent higher than those who are not SHRM certified.

» **SHRM-certified HR professionals feel better about their careers.** SHRM-certified HR professionals have 30 percent higher commitment to the profession of HR and 17 percent greater likelihood of pride in the quality of work they have produced. They also report high career satisfaction at a significantly higher rate (+22 percent) than noncertified professionals.

» **SHRM-certified professionals have fewer concerns about job security.**
Only 4 percent of SHRM-certified HR professionals reported being "very
concerned" about their job security, while 22 percent of noncertified HR
professionals reported feeling this way.

» **SHRM-certified professionals feel respected amongst peers.** Ninety-
two percent of SHRM-certified HR professionals report feelings of
respect amongst professionals and peers. Seventy-nine percent
of SHRM-certified HR professionals were offered opportunities to take
on higher levels of responsibility and reported a higher likelihood (25
percent) of leading a project team.

Organizational Benefit from SHRM Certification

HR professionals are not the only beneficiaries of a SHRM-CP or SHRM-SCP
certification. SHRM research shows that the HR department and the entire
organization can gain tangible and valuable advantages too. Once you set your
certification goal, use these four points to demonstrate why your manager and
organization should support your efforts to prepare for and attain certification.

SHRM research conducted in 2022 showed there are four top ways your organization will benefit from your SHRM-CP or your SHRM-SCP certification:

» **Your HR knowledge will be current and relevant.** Ninety-two percent
of SHRM-certified HR professionals agree they have current and up-to-
date information on HR best practices. You will have access to extensive
resources through SHRM, including SHRM news articles, toolkits, and
other resources on the shrm.org website that you can apply to your
organization. Attaining and maintaining your credential means you will be
ready to take on more challenging responsibilities.

» **You will continue to learn practical skills that will positively impact
your job.** SHRM-certified professionals complete almost twice as many
learning and development activities per year as noncertified professionals. After becoming certified, you will engage in activities like attending
conferences, coaching, and networking—so the learning never stops. You
will be applying concepts, using judgment, and understanding HR's best
practices for both day-to-day and unexpected scenarios. Eighty percent
of all HR professionals agree SHRM certification helps with maintaining
compliance with the law as well.

» **You will be better prepared for business challenges.** Growing the influence of HR leaders through certification is a worthwhile investment that also improves your organization's reputation as one that takes HR seriously. Just as a certified project management professional (PMP) is trusted to know how to successfully lead projects and people, you will earn the same type of trust with your SHRM-CP or SHRM-SCP credential. The decisions you make will positively affect your organization. In fact, 63 percent of SHRM-certified HR professionals report their decisions impacted their organization versus 41 percent of noncertified HR professionals.

» **Your knowledge and skills will be globally applicable and universally recognized.** Earning a SHRM credential will give you the confidence and ability to use the knowledge and skills you have acquired anywhere in your organization, now and in the future. The SHRM BASK is the foundation of your SHRM credential. SHRM regularly conducts global research to validate and update the SHRM BASK so it remains relevant and reflects the future of HR. SHRM research shows that SHRM-certified HR professionals report levels of respect from their professional colleagues and peers at a higher rate than noncertified counterparts. Eighty-six percent of HR professionals believe SHRM Certification adds to the overall credibility of an HR department.

Chapter 1

The Exams and What They Test

An Overview of the SHRM Body of Applied Skills and Knowledge (SHRM BASK), the Two Exams, and Accreditation

Strive not to be a success, but rather to be of value.

—*Albert Einstein*

The SHRM certification exams test your capabilities in both aspects of HR practice—applied skills and knowledge—that are required for effective job performance. The exams are based upon the core set of applied skills and knowledge outlined in the SHRM BASK. SHRM certification exams are accredited by the Buros Center for Testing at University of Nebraska–Lincoln.

A product of rigorous research involving thousands of HR professionals, the SHRM BASK identifies nine key behavioral competencies and 14 HR functional areas that are critical to the success of any HR professional. The SHRM BASK will be your study outline as you prepare for your exam (see Figure 1.1).

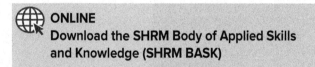

ONLINE
Download the SHRM Body of Applied Skills and Knowledge (SHRM BASK)

https://www.shrm.org/credentials/certification/exam-preparation/body-of-applied-skills-and-knowledge

Figure 1.1. Know Your SHRM BASK!

For Examinees Who Test Outside of the United States

The SHRM BASK includes one functional area that covers US employment laws and regulations—residing in the Workplace HR Expertise functional area. However, questions in this functional area do not appear on exams for examinees who reside *and* take an exam outside of the United States. If you reside and take your exam outside of the United States, you will still have the same number of scored and nonscored items on your exam—134 questions; however, all questions from the US Employment Law and Regulations functional area will be removed and replaced with items from other sections of the SHRM BASK that are globally applicable. There are no changes to the questions on the exams that fall under the nine behavioral competencies and 13 remaining functional areas.

SNAPSHOT
What Accreditation Is and Why It Matters

Accreditation for a credentialing program provides important corroboration of the program's quality and rigor as determined by an independent, qualified third party against a set of established standard of quality measured by the testing industry. The SHRM-CP and SHRM-SCP are accredited by the Buros Center for Testing at the University of Nebraska–Lincoln.

The Buros Center evaluates the psychometric quality of credentialing testing programs like SHRM's testing program. The center conducts a general audit of the program's processes and procedures along with a yearly, focused evaluation of specific testing windows within the program. SHRM participates in both types of accreditation audit—the periodic general audit and the annual, focused testing-year evaluation.

Buros reviews SHRM's policies and procedures to ensure the SHRM-CP and SHRM-SCP maintain the required quality standards that apply to testing programs. Its review is based on the extent to which SHRM's testing program demonstrates that it meets the Buros Standards for Accreditation of Testing Programs. At the end of each audit phase, Buros provides evidence that the SHRM-CP and SHRM-SCP exams adhere to those standards, along with ways in which the policies or procedures could be modified or improved to meet or address emerging expectations of the professional community.

The Buros standards are periodically updated to reflect current guidelines from the testing community. In particular, the center's standards are highly consistent with the 2014 Standards for Educational and Psychological Testing, jointly published by the American Educational Research Association (AERA), the American Psychological Association (APA), and the National Council on Measurement in Education (NCME). The Buros National Advisory Council unanimously approved its revised standards in June 2017. SHRM provides information annually to maintain its accreditation for the SHRM-CP and SHRM-SCP certifications.

Recognized by HR Employers

SHRM certification is the fastest-growing program in the HR certification community. More than 30,500 applicants sought SHRM certification in 2020, and more than half of job postings listed SHRM credential holders as preferred applicants.

Meets the Highest Standards

The SHRM-CP and SHRM-SCP exams are accredited by the Buros Center for Testing, the global leader in evaluating the psychometric quality of examinations. They are an independent body that reviews SHRM policies and procedures to ensure a standard of quality as measured by testing industry professionals.

Fueled by HR Competencies

SHRM certification is powered by the SHRM BASK®, which was developed and validated by more than 40,000 HR professionals. Nine out of ten non-HR business executives view competencies as important for overall HR department success.

Engineered by Experts

Each year, approximately 1,000 subject matter experts from around the world come together over the course of 28 workshops to develop new items for SHRM certification exams. SHRM certification exam development is led by top-notch, professionally trained exam development experts with an average of thirty years of experience.

Raises the Global Standards

SHRM certification has worldwide reach with credential-holders in 105 countries. SHRM's Certification Commission ensures the quality and impartiality of the SHRM certification program.

Built with Your Future in Mind

SHRM's competency-based certification was designed to transport you across 100 percent of your HR career. With more than 110,000 educational programs and a network of over 3,100+ providers, SHRM supports you through recertification and lifelong professional development in an ever-changing industry.

Figure 1.2. Six Things You Should Know About SHRM Certification

Two Certification Exams and Eligibility

SHRM offers two levels of certification: the SHRM-CP and the SHRM-SCP. You should choose the exam level that best matches your job duties and then cross-check the eligibility table (Table 1.1) to determine whether you meet the specific eligibility requirements for the exam level you selected.

Which exam you take depends on which certification aligns most closely with your job responsibilities and level of experience and whether you meet the specific eligibility requirements.

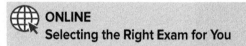
ONLINE
Selecting the Right Exam for You

Not sure which exam to take? Use the interactive wizard on the certification website to help you determine which credential is right for you. After answering a series of questions about your career level, education, and types of experience, you will receive a recommendation about which certification to pursue. To learn more, go to the following webpage:

https://www.shrm.org/credentials/certification/which-shrm-certification

If you are still not sure which SHRM certification exam to take even after reviewing the descriptions of the exams, we recommend that you start with the SHRM-CP and then work to pass the SHRM-SCP later in your career.

How to Apply

SHRM offers both certification exams during two testing windows every year. The first window is from May 1 to July 15, and the second window is from December 1 to February 15. Examinees can choose to take the exam in person at one of more than 500 Prometric testing centers across more than 180 countries, or you can choose to take it via live remote proctoring.

Once you have decided which exam to take, register to take the exam on the SHRM website anytime between the applications accepted starting date and the standard application deadline.

TABLE 1.1. SHRM-CP and SHRM-SCP Eligibility

 **SHRM Certified Professional (SHRM-CP)**

- The SHRM-CP certification is intended for individuals who perform general HR or HR-related duties, or for currently enrolled students and individuals pursuing a career in Human Resource Management.
- Candidates for the SHRM-CP certification are not required to hold an HR title and do not need a degree or previous HR experience to apply; however, a basic working knowledge of HR practices and principles or a degree from an Academically Aligned program is recommended.
- The SHRM-CP exam is designed to assess the competency level of HR at the operational level. This level includes implementing policies, supporting day-to-day HR functions, or serving as an HR point of contact for staff and stakeholders.
- Refer to the SHRM BASK for detailed information on proficiency standards for this credential (i.e., Proficiency Indicators only for All HR Professionals).

 **SHRM Senior Certified Professional (SHRM-SCP)**

- The SHRM-SCP certification is for individuals who have a work history of at least **three years performing strategic level HR or HR-related duties,** or for SHRM-CP credential holders who have held the credential for at least three years and are working in, or are in the process of transitioning to, a strategic level role.
- Candidates for the SHRM-SCP certification are not required to hold an HR title and do not need a degree to apply.
- The SHRM-SCP exam is designed to assess the competency level of those who engage in HR work at the strategic level. Work at this level includes duties such as developing HR policies and/or procedures, overseeing the execution of integrated HR operations, directing an entire HR enterprise, or leading the alignment of HR strategies to organizational goals.
- Applicants must be able to demonstrate that they devoted at least 1,000 hours per calendar year (Jan.–Dec.) to strategic-level HR or HR-related work.
  - More than 1,000 hours in a calendar year does not equate to more than one year of experience.
  - Part-time work qualifies as long as the 1,000-hour per calendar year standard is met.
  - Experience may be either salaried or hourly.
- Individuals who are HR consultants may demonstrate qualifying experience through the HR or HR-related duties they perform for their clients. Contracted hours must meet the 1,000-hour standard.
- Refer to the SHRM BASK for detailed information on proficiency standards for this credential (i.e., Proficiency Indicators for All HR Professionals and for Advanced HR Professionals).

Examinees who apply by the early-bird application deadline or who are SHRM members receive a reduced exam fee. Note that exam applications apply for specific testing windows; once you have applied, transferring to the next testing windows is possible for an additional fee.

To learn more about the benefits of SHRM Memberships and receive discounts on the SHRM Learning System, the SHRM Certification exams, and much more, navigate to this link: https://www.shrm.org/membership.

To apply, you must

1. Apply online (https://www.shrm.org/credentials/certification).

2. Create a user account.

3. Select which level exam you want to take.

4. Complete the application form and sign the SHRM Certification Candidate Agreement.

5. Pay the application fee.

6. Once you receive your Authorization-to-Test (ATT) letter, schedule your exam directly through SHRM's test delivery vendor (https://www. prometric.com/shrm). Your ATT letter will outline several ways to schedule your exam and select your testing location and modality (test in person or via remote proctoring).

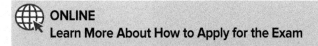

ONLINE
Learn More About How to Apply for the Exam

https://www.shrm.org/credentials/certification/
exam-options-fees

Chapter 2

Exam Structure and Question Types

Energy and persistence conquer all things.

—Benjamin Franklin

An important part of preparing yourself for the test is knowing what kinds of questions you will be asked and how the test is structured and administered.

The structure and administration of the SHRM-CP and SHRM-SCP exams are nearly identical. They have the same number of questions (134), the same question structure, and the same amount of exam time (3 hours and 40 minutes). Because of this similarity between exams, most of the advice provided in this book will be relevant to both exams. The largest difference is in the underlying conceptual framework of questions asked—the SHRM-CP focuses on the operational level, while the SHRM-SCP is more focused on strategy and effectively managing an HR department. These differences in conceptual framework are detailed in the SHRM BASK, outlined as *proficiency indicators*, specific to **All HR Professionals** or **Advanced HR Professionals**.

Figure 2.1 outlines an example of the talent acquisition functional area found within the people knowledge domain. In addition to a brief description of the functional area, a listing of *key concepts* details specific processes, approaches, knowledge, frameworks, and so on that fall into those content areas. Figure 2.2 takes that a step further with the *proficiency indicators*. These define prominent practices at the *All HR Professionals* level (designed for *operational* level practitioners), or at the *Advanced HR Professionals* level (designed for *strategic* level practitioners).

Recall that the SHRM BASK is based on a global practice analysis of the HR profession and provides the basis for developing the SHRM certification exams. The test blueprint is derived from the SHRM BASK. It provides the framework that specifies how many questions are included on each exam from each of the SHRM BASK's nine behavioral competencies and 14 HR knowledge areas (or

FUNCTIONAL AREAS | PEOPLE KNOWLEDGE DOMAIN | TALENT ACQUISITION

Talent Acquisition

Talent Acquisition encompasses the activities involved in identifying, attracting and building a workforce that meets the needs of the organization.

Key Concepts
- ▷ Methods for creating and maintaining a positive employee value proposition (EVP) and employment brand
  - ▷ Examples include culture; opportunity for growth; purpose; varied work assignments
- ▷ Job analysis and identification of job requirements
  - ▷ Examples include job requirements and qualifications; task inventory analysis; critical incident technique; position analysis questionnaire
- ▷ Methods for external and internal sourcing and recruiting
  - ▷ Examples include job ads; career fairs; social media; college/university relationships; talent pipelines; internal job postings; employee referrals
- ▷ Methods for selection assessment
  - ▷ Examples include ability; job knowledge; personality tests; assessment centers; individual or panel interviews
- ▷ Employment categories
  - ▷ Examples include full time; part time; contract; temporary workers; interns
- ▷ Job offer contingencies
  - ▷ Examples include background investigations; credit checks; physical or psychological evaluations
- ▷ Job offer negotiations
  - ▷ Examples include salary; relocation assistance; telecommuting; variable job share
- ▷ Approaches to employee onboarding
  - ▷ Examples include orientation; buddy system; personalization
- ▷ Talent acquisition metrics
  - ▷ Examples include cost per hire; time to fill; applicant-to-interview-to-offer ratio; candidate yield from proactive sourcing
- ▷ Talent acquisition technologies
  - ▷ Examples include applicant tracking system (ATS); chatbots; artificial intelligence resume screening; social media to identify passive talent
- ▷ Methods for supporting a positive candidate experience
  - ▷ Examples include streamlined application process; limited rounds of interviews; fair consideration of applicant's time; frequent communication

Figure 2.1. SHRM BASK Example: Talent Acquisition Key Concepts

FUNCTIONAL AREAS | PEOPLE KNOWLEDGE DOMAIN | TALENT ACQUISITION

PROFICIENCY INDICATORS FOR ALL HR PROFESSIONALS
- ▷ Understands the talent needs of the organization or business unit.
- ▷ Uses a wide variety of talent sources and recruiting methods to attract a qualified and diverse pool of applicants.
- ▷ Uses technology to support effective and efficient approaches to sourcing and recruiting employees.
- ▷ Promotes and uses the EVP and employment brand for sourcing and recruiting applicants.
- ▷ Uses the most appropriate hiring methods and assessments to evaluate a candidate's technical skills, organizational fit and alignment with the organization's competency needs based on job requirements.
- ▷ Conducts appropriate pre-employment screening.
- ▷ Implements effective onboarding and orientation programs for new employees.
- ▷ Designs job descriptions to meet the organization's resource needs.
- ▷ Complies with local and country-specific laws and regulations governing talent acquisition (such as avoiding illegal interview questions).
- ▷ Advises and coaches hiring managers on best practices related to job descriptions, interviews, onboarding and candidate experience.

FOR ADVANCED HR PROFESSIONALS
- ▷ Analyzes staffing levels and projections to forecast workforce needs.
- ▷ Develops strategies for sourcing and acquiring a workforce that meets the organization's needs.
- ▷ Establishes an EVP and employment brand that supports recruitment of high-quality job applicants.
- ▷ Designs and oversees effective strategies for sourcing, recruiting and evaluating qualified job candidates.
- ▷ Designs and oversees employee onboarding processes.
- ▷ Designs and oversees valid and systematic programs for assessing the effectiveness of talent acquisition activities that meet the organization's needs.

Figure 2.2. SHRM BASK Example: Talent Acquisition Proficiency Indicators

13 HR knowledge areas for candidates taking the exams outside of the United States, as explained in Chapter 1).

Two item types comprise the SHRM certification exams: knowledge items (KIs) and situational judgment items (SJIs).

 QUICK TIP

Looking for practice items from prior SHRM exams? To see examples of real, previously administered exam questions, check out the practice test in Appendix 2. It contains KIs and SJIs that appeared on SHRM certification tests in the recent years and provides a realistic preview of what you can expect operational exam questions to look like in format, structure, and content. Keep in mind that none of the items on this or any practice test will appear on the operational exam you take on test day.

Additionally, check out the SHRM-CP and SHRM-SCP workbooks for additional unique SHRM practice questions.

Knowledge Items

Knowledge items are **stand-alone, multiple-choice items** that test a single piece of knowledge or application of knowledge. KIs test your knowledge of key concepts (as identified by the SHRM BASK). Knowledge items have only one, irrefutably correct response option called the *key*. Each knowledge item is linked to a specific source and has a rationale that explains why it is the only correct answer (key).

Knowledge items are further divided into two types:

» HR-specific knowledge items (KIs) cover key concept topics associated with the 14 HR functional areas defined in the SHRM BASK.

» Foundational knowledge items (FKIs) cover the key concepts that are considered foundational to each of the nine behavioral competencies.

There are a total of **80 knowledge items** on the SHRM exams, including both KIs and FKIs.

Each knowledge item is classified according to the depth of knowledge, or level of understanding or application, required to answer it. There are four levels in the depth of knowledge framework: (1) recall, (2) understanding, (3) problem-solving, and (4) critical evaluation. Level 1 recall questions make up approximately 10 percent of the knowledge items on the SHRM certification exams, while higher level questions make up the remaining 90 percent of knowledge items. Both KIs and FKIs include items written across the four levels in the depth of knowledge framework.

Basic Level: Recall Questions

Recall questions represent the base of the framework. They are just at the surface of cognitive complexity. They serve an important purpose by requiring test takers to access and recite information stored in their brains.

Recall questions may ask the test taker to define a specific term, or they may supply a definition and ask the test taker to identify the term being defined.

Following is an example of a recall question and answer that could appear on a SHRM exam:

> **Q**: What change management model follows the pattern of "unfreeze, change, refreeze"?
>
> **A**: Lewin's Model

Next Level: Understanding Questions

The slightly more rigorous *understanding* questions act as a shovel to break through the Level 1 recall surface. They require test takers to comprehend information, compare two things, translate by applying knowledge, or interpret a concept to apply it. In other words, they assess one's ability to recognize how HR concepts and terms manifest themselves in the workplace.

Understanding questions are designed to ensure that candidates who pass the exam are both knowledgeable and possess the skills and abilities required to be a competent HR professional.

Following is an example of an understanding question and answer that mirrors the operational exam content and structure:

> **Q**: During a board meeting, a leader at a technology company describes a potential crisis that threatens the company's ability to operate. This action implements which step in Kotter's eight-step change management model?
>
> **A**: Creating a sense of urgency

To answer this question, the test taker needs to remember all the steps in Kotter's model and how to apply them properly.

High Level: Problem-Solving Questions

Problem-solving questions require test takers to apply their knowledge to develop a solution to a problem, which is something HR professionals do every day. To select the correct answer, one must draw on one's knowledge and understanding of many different concepts and strategies, which is more cognitively demanding than the recall of information.

Following is an example of a problem-solving question and answer that mirrors the operational exam content and structure:

> **Q**: After a recent layoff, the CEO announces plans to restructure the organization. Which action should leadership take first to help hesitant employees adjust to the changes?

> **A**: Identify strong senior sponsorship for the change.

The problem presented in this question is the employees' hesitation. To answer, the test taker needs to identify the action that will most effectively help them overcome it.

The problem presented in this question is the employees' hesitation. To answer, the test taker needs to identify the action that will most effectively help them overcome it.

Highest Level: Critical Evaluation Questions

Critical evaluation questions, which ask test takers to analyze information to predict an outcome, are the most challenging. A competent HR professional uses the ability to predict outcomes to guide business strategy and execution.

Following is an example of a critical evaluation question that mirrors the operational exam content and structure:

> **Q**: During a change management initiative, which outcome is most likely to happen if an organization focuses only on the bottom line?

> **A**: The impacts of the change to the individuals currently working in the organization are overlooked.

Here, the test taker must have knowledge of change management initiatives and how organizations choose to implement them. Using that knowledge, the HR professional should recommend ways to minimize any negative effects.

Situational Judgment Items

In contrast, situational judgment items (SJIs) are scenario-based question sets (numbering two to three questions per scenario) that present realistic situations that are likely to occur in workplaces throughout the world and are similar to what many HR professionals have likely experienced during their careers. Based on the scenario presented, SJIs ask test takers to consider the problem presented in the question within the context of the situation, and then select the best or most effective course of action to take from the available response options.

Like knowledge items, each SJI has four response options from which to choose. However, SJIs test decision-making and judgment skills—not application of knowledge. SJIs allow you to use what you know from experiences in your day-to-day professional life to show you know how to make competent judgments and decisions. Therefore, the response options range from the most effective to the least effective course of action.

 QUICK TIP

Keep in mind, when approaching knowledge items, there is one correct response and three incorrect responses. When approaching situational judgment items, each response option exists on a range of effective to ineffective behaviors. You will select the response option that you assess to be the most effective course of action to take, given the options presented.

When selecting your answer, consider that more than one of the possible responses might be effective, but only one will be the *best* or *most effective* course of action based on the situation and the decision of the panel of SHRM-certified HR professionals.

It is important to note that SJIs do not test *your company's* approach, *your own* approach, or *your industry's* approach. Nor do they test how to follow specific laws or HR policies. They test what competent behavior looks like in action as defined by the proficiency indicators in the SHRM BASK for each of the nine behavioral competencies.

There are **54 SJIs** on the SHRM exams.

HR professionals from many countries around the world provide the raw material for situational judgment items in the form of critical incident documentation.

Critical incidents are drawn from real-life situations that are likely to be common occurrences in workplaces in every country across the world. HR professionals also provide the action they took to solve or overcome the situation, along with multiple alternative courses of action that could have been taken. Possible actions range from very effective to very ineffective. These become the basis for the response options. Figure 2.3 depicts the entire SJI development process.

> ## QUICK TIP
>
> It may be helpful to streamline your thinking about SJIs to remove some of the mystery that accompanies this item type. Think about SJIs this way: they require you to do nothing different than what you do every day at work. Something happens, you assess the situation to figure out what occurred, you decide the best course of action to address the situation, and then you act by implementing that best course of action.

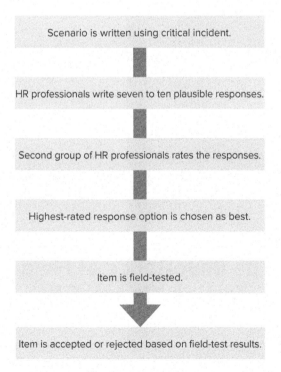

Scenario is written using critical incident.

HR professionals write seven to ten plausible responses.

Second group of HR professionals rates the responses.

Highest-rated response option is chosen as best.

Item is field-tested.

Item is accepted or rejected based on field-test results.

Figure 2.3. How Situational Judgment Items (SJIs) Are Created

How SHRM Determines the Best Response to an SJI

Before SJIs are administered on a SHRM exam, scoring panels composed of seasoned global SHRM-certified HR professionals rate the possible responses to identify the best or most effective response, which is called the key. At this stage in the review process, these teams review eight to ten possible response options and assign to each a numeric equivalent ranging from the most effective response to least effective response. Statistical analysis of effectiveness ratings then determines the key.

Panelists use the proficiency indicators in the SHRM BASK for each of the nine behavioral competencies when rating the effectiveness of each response on the scale from most effective to least effective. Therefore, it is important to be well-acquainted with the proficiency indicators for the nine behavioral competencies.

Because the best response is based on numerous expert judgment ratings, there are no rationales for SJI correct responses. The aggregated judgments of expert panelists alone serve as validation for the key.

 QUICK TIP

Knowledge items are based on primary sources or reference materials (HR textbooks, HR research articles, etc.). A listing of sources can be found in Appendix A of the SHRM BASK.

Situational judgment items are based on HR expert rater judgment, combined with other rater's judgments, to reach consensus on the singular most effective course of action.

The Importance of Field-Testing KIs and SJIs

Before a KI or an SJI can be part of the scored, operational test-item set, each one must first be subjected to field testing (also known as pilot testing), as an unscored question. *Field test items*, including both KIs and SJIs, are used to determine the quality of an item. Quality measures are calculated after

SNAPSHOT

SHRM's certification exams use situational judgment items (SJIs) to assess abilities defined in the nine behavioral competencies in the SHRM BASK. For the HR profession, behaving competently is inextricably linked to HR knowledge. Thus, SJIs allow certification candidates to use what they know to demonstrate how to behave competently in a given situation.

When you answer SJIs, try:

1. Reflecting on what occurs in the workplace day in and day out.

    How does your behavior affect the outcome of a given situation at work? For example, deciding to create a business continuity plan to safeguard the organization from risk.

2. Deciding what HR role to perform.

    Does a situation call for HR to lead ethically, communicate, consult, manage relationships, or perform another essential role primarily?

3. Thinking of it like riding a bicycle or driving a car.

    While answering KIs might be comparable to knowing the rules of the road, SJIs require you to operate the bicycle or car competently on the road.

hundreds of examinees answer the item as a field test item. This helps determine the overall quality and eligibility of an item *to become* a scored item on a future SHRM-CP or SHRM-SCP exam.

Taken as a group, examinee responses to field test questions serve two purposes. First, they help SHRM identify items that are possible additions to future exams without affecting your test results. Second, they support growth of the certification program by assessing item quality. These factors determine the field test item's eligibility to be retained in the item bank and to be placed on a future test form. If a field test item is viable, as determined by a required set of standards, only then does the item move from field test status to operational status. If it does not meet quality standards, the item is not eligible to become a scored item or be used on a future test form.

Only the 110 operational set of KIs and SJIs are scored and contribute to a pass or fail decision. Currently, there are 24 field test questions out of the 134 total items on each exam. Field test items are randomly mixed with other items and are not scored.

After the field test items are pretested, SHRM analyzes each item's statistical quality. Only those questions that meet the performance standards become scored items on future exams. Each test form of 134 items changes every time an exam administration occurs.

 QUICK TIP

Field test items appear randomly throughout the exam. While these questions do not count against your total score, they are indiscernible from scored items. Therefore, you should attempt to answer all the questions on the test.

If you don't know the answer to a question, do your best to reason through it and answer the question to the best of your ability.

Do not skip any questions!

SHRM's Item-Writing Methodology

Each year, approximately 1,000 SHRM-certified HR subject matter experts from around the world come together over the course of 28 workshops to develop, edit, review, and refine new field test-eligible items for SHRM certification exams.

SHRM certification exam development is led by top-notch, professionally trained exam development experts who guide the subject matter experts through the process of drafting exam items. After the team drafts exam items, the items go through several rounds of review to validate that the content and key are correct, the item is applicable to the field of HR, and the item does not contain bias or cultural sensitivity issues.

It is also important to understand there are no SHRM answers. As we've discussed, SHRM-certified HR professionals write, edit, review, and select correct answers for the test questions. Correct answers are validated by these subject matter experts using accessible resources based on factual HR knowledge for KIs and an HR expert rater agreement for SJIs. The SHRM staff provides expertise in test development, not HR subject-matter expertise, and SHRM staff does not draft content that supersedes the HR expert review stages.

SHRM-CP and SHRM-SCP Exam Structure

Both the SHRM-CP and SHRM-SCP certification exams consist of 134 questions. Each exam is broken into two equal halves containing 67 questions. Each half is divided into three sections: first, a section of 20 KIs and FKIs; then a section of 27 SJIs; and finally, another section of 20 KIs and FKIs (Figure 2.4).

First Half
(67 questions)

20 KIs/FKIs
27 SJIs
20 KIs/FKIs

Second Half
(67 questions)

20 KIs/FKIs
27 SJIs
20 KIs/FKIs

Figure 2.4. Exam Structure

Examinees must complete the first half of an exam before moving on to the second half. Ensure that you respond to *all* of the questions before moving on to a new section or completing the exam. Questions left blank are counted as an incorrect response and can negatively affect your final score. Once an examinee begins the second half, the examinee cannot return to the first half to review questions or change answers.

Exam Timing

The total exam appointment time is four hours, which includes three hours and 40 minutes of testing time for the exam itself. The exam time is broken down into the following segments:

Introduction (including the confidentiality reminder)—four minutes

Tutorial—eight minutes

Exam Half 1—Up to one hour and fifty minutes

Exam Half 2—Up to one hour and fifty minutes

Survey—six minutes

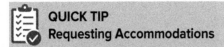

QUICK TIP
Requesting Accommodations

You will have approximately ninety-eight seconds per exam question. Leverage your time wisely knowing SJIs present a larger reading load—making up 40 percent of the overall exam. Pace yourself, take your time, and use that time appropriately!

If you are concerned you need more time and you would like to request an accommodation, see Chapter 10 on steps to apply.

There are a few transition screens throughout the exam that account for the remaining minutes. Remember that you can take an unscheduled break of up to 15 minutes, even though a break is not included in the total time. Gauge your time as you near the end of the first section. If you reach question 60 and you still have a half hour left, plan to take a break before ending section one. Tell the proctor before you take your break that you are taking a break. For remote testers, do this using the chat feature. When you take your break, the exam clock will continue to run.

See Chapter 11 for more information about how to strategically use your break time.

Each section shows a countdown timer on the screen, so you can keep track of how much time you have left. Also, each section is separate and timed independently. Minutes do not roll over. For instance, if you spend less time in the tutorial, those extra minutes are not rolled over to the first exam half.

Exam Items by Content and Item Type

The distribution of items with respect to content and item type is essentially the same for both the SHRM-CP and SHRM-SCP exams. About half of the items on each exam are allocated across the three behavioral competency clusters, and the other half are allocated across the three HR knowledge domains (see Figure 2.5). Approximately 40 percent of the items on each exam are

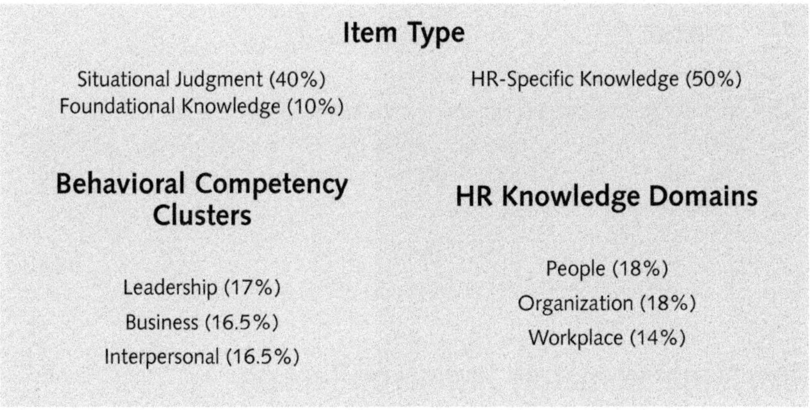

Item Type

Situational Judgment (40%)   HR-Specific Knowledge (50%)
Foundational Knowledge (10%)

Behavioral Competency Clusters

HR Knowledge Domains

Leadership (17%)

People (18%)
Organization (18%)
Workplace (14%)

Business (16.5%)

Interpersonal (16.5%)

Figure 2.5. Distribution of Exam Items by Content and Exam Type

situational judgment items, and the remainder are stand-alone items measuring either knowledge that is foundational to the behavioral competencies (10%) or HR-specific knowledge (50%).

How the Exams Are Administered

The SHRM-CP and SHRM-SCP exams are administered via computer-based testing. Examinees can take an exam either in-person at a highly secure Prometric testing center or virtually using live remote proctoring. *Live remote proctoring* means the testing session is monitored by a qualified proctor through audio-video and screen-share feed in real time.

Once your exam application has been accepted for a testing window, you will schedule your exam on the Prometric website or by calling Prometric directly. When scheduling your exam, you will decide whether to take your exam in-person at a testing center or via live remote proctoring.

Before you schedule your exam via remote proctoring, run the system readiness check to verify that your computer meets the minimum system requirements. In addition, think carefully about your needs and the testing experience that you think will work best for you. Consider why remote proctored testing might be a good option for you and why it might not be the best fit. For example, if your computer does not meet the minimum system requirements or you do not have access to a stable internet connection, live remote proctoring is not a good option for you. Use the following questions and answers as a start to guide your choice. You can also read about what to expect on exam day for each mode in Chapter 11.

ONLINE

From website below, complete Prometric's system readiness check to determine whether your operating system is compatible to install and run the ProProctor™ application so that you can take a remotely proctored exam:

https://rpcandidate.prometric.com/

Why Might Remotely-Proctored Testing Be a Good Option?

There are many reasons people choose to test remotely. One of these reasons might fit your circumstances:

» Testing in a familiar place helps put you at ease.

» The nearest test center is farther away than you wish to travel.

» The convenience of testing anytime and anywhere gives you more control over your experience.

» There are no in-person seats available at the time you want to test.

Why Might Remotely-Proctored Testing NOT Be a Good Option?

Remote-proctored testing isn't for everyone. When you take a SHRM certification exam via remote proctoring, your home or office *becomes* the testing center. This means you are responsible for ensuring the security of your exam as well as providing the computer and internet connection to complete the exam. Here are some strong reasons why remote proctoring might *not* be the best option for you:

» You do not have access to a computer that meets Prometric's system requirements.

» You do not have a strong, stable internet connection.

» You do not have a quiet, private room (with a door that closes) at your home or office to take the exam.

» You want to have immediate access to an in-person test center administrator in case something goes wrong with your exam.

 ONLINE

Learn more about taking a SHRM-CP or SHRM-SCP exam from Prometric by visiting

https://www.prometric.com/SHRM

Chapter 3

Exam Scoring

*Success isn't about the end result, it's about
what you learn along the way.*

—Vera Wang

SHRM uses a rigorous scoring process for certification exams, which includes third-party independent validation and verification. Passing scores are set using a best-practice that is commonly used procedure for high-stakes certification and licensing exams. This is known as setting the performance standard.

Your individual performance will be measured against the predetermined standard, not against that of other people taking the test. To maintain the integrity of the SHRM Certification Program, the SHRM Certification Commission evaluates the scoring standard recommendations and ensures the technical quality of all test-scoring practices.

After you have finished the test, the system calculates a Pass/Did Not Pass result, posts a statement on your screen, and emails the Pass/Did Not Pass result to the email address you used when scheduling your testing appointment. You will receive the official score report about two to three weeks after you take the test. The official score report will be posted to your SHRM Certification account in the certification portal.

How the Exams Are Scored

Many candidates ask SHRM how the SHRM-CP and SHRM-SCP certification examinations are scored, and how those scores are reported to examinees. The most frequently asked questions include the following:

» Why is 200 the passing score when the exam has 134 questions?

» Do I have to earn the maximum score to pass the exam?

>> What is the number of questions I must answer correctly to pass the exam?

>> What is the number of questions I must answer correctly in the SHRM Learning System to know if I will pass the exam?

To keep the SHRM certification exams up-to-date and fair, during every testing window, we add and remove questions. Before a new question is used, it is first pretested (also called field-testing) with real examinees. We do that by mixing 24 unscored field test questions into each exam. Examinees answer the field test questions, but answers to field test questions are not part of the pass decision. In other words, of the 134 questions on the exam that you answer, 110 are used to calculate your score; the 24 field test items do not count. Because there is no way for you to know which questions count toward your score and which do not, it is important to do your best on all test items.

Now, let's talk about how SHRM sets the passing scores for the SHRM certification exams. SHRM employs best-practice procedures most commonly used for setting performance standards for certification and licensure exams. During a multiday evaluation process, a panel of experienced HR professionals evaluates the exam questions to determine how difficult they are for a candidate who is just-qualified or minimally qualified at the appropriate level: SHRM-CP (for those in operational roles) or SHRM-SCP (for those in strategic roles).

Raw Scores and Scaled Scores

The SHRM-CP and SHRM-SCP exams have 134 questions, and 110 of them are used to calculate your score. After you take the test, you will have a *raw score* of 0–110 correctly selected responses (keys), but the score we report to you is *on a scale* of 120–200, with passing set at 200—this is known as your *scaled score*.

It is a common and best practice in standardized testing to place the number of questions answered correctly on a scale (scaled score), rather than to simply report to the examinee the number of questions answered correctly (raw score). You may be familiar with this process if you have taken the SAT or ACT for college, the GRE for graduate school, or the GMAT for a master's degree in business administration. The scores for these exams range from 400–1600 for the SAT, 1–36 for the ACT, 130–170 for the GRE, and 200–800 for the GMAT. Just like on the SHRM-CP and SHRM-SCP exams, the numbers of questions on these tests differ from their reported scores.

What Does a 200 Score Mean?

For the SHRM exams, 200 is not necessarily a perfect score—it is the passing score. We do not report scaled scores above 200 because anyone who passes the SHRM-CP or SHRM-SCP exam is considered to have achieved the competency level required to earn certification.

Whether you passed either exam by one question or by many, you will receive a scaled score of 200. Instead of simply providing a Pass/Did Not Pass result, SHRM provides all examinees with a score report that shows on a graph how well they did in each of three competency clusters and in each of three knowledge domains. This additional information can aid test takers in evaluating their strengths and weaknesses. Unsuccessful examinees have a numerical score to find out how close they were to being successful, plus a descriptive graphic to help them make appropriate choices about how to prepare for future exams. For successful examinees, the score report serves as feedback on their performance and can help guide their recertification plans and professional development activities.

SHRM exam scores are also equated across administrations—meaning there are anchor items to ensure that a candidate would achieve a comparable score regardless of which form of the test they are administered in any given testing window or appointment. Equating is one reason why we cannot state the number of questions one needs to answer correctly to get a passing score. The number of correct questions you need to pass your exam form may differ slightly from the number of correct questions another examinee needs to pass an exam form administered during another testing window. These fluctuations are addressed through the equating process to make each test administration equivalent to any other testing experience on the same exam in terms of results.

SHRM certification test takers are not compared against each other—that is, the exams are not scored on what is commonly known as a curve. (In technical terms, the exams are not *normed*.) If everyone who takes their test meets the knowledge and competency standards, everyone will pass. The opposite is also true. If no one who takes the test meets the knowledge and competency standards, no one will pass

If You Don't Pass

Do not feel discouraged if you do not pass the certification exam. It is a very challenging exam, and between 30 percent and 45 percent of exam takers do not pass on the first try. Whether you pass or fail, you will receive an official score report uploaded to your SHRM portal following notification from SHRM that your score report is available.

Leverage the information on your score report and utilize the SHRM BASK to revisit the knowledge domains or behavioral competencies and dig deeper into the key concepts and proficiency indicators. If you are unsuccessful in your attempt, look to additional SHRM offerings like the SHRM-CP or SHRM-SCP workbooks and the SHRM Learning System for a comprehensive preparation experience and additional practice with SHRM-developed study questions.

View the experience as a learning opportunity and use the information in your score report to refocus or reengineer a study plan that will help you prepare for retaking the SHRM-CP or SHRM-SCP exam. You can retake the exam in a future testing window by completing a new application and paying the exam fee.

Examinees who do not pass the exam are prohibited from retaking the exam within the same testing window.

Part 2

Study for Success

A journey of a thousand miles begins with a single step.

–Chinese Proverb

The better you plan your study journey, the more pleasant your overall preparation experience will be. To succeed on the SHRM-CP or SHRM-SCP exam, you have to know the subject matter that is being tested: the competencies and knowledge outlined in the SHRM BASK. There are two key ingredients. First, your experience as an HR professional is key to mastering knowledge and best-practice behavior to solve problems. Second, support your chances for success on the exam by creating a carefully designed and implemented study plan.

Start with your HR experience. Think about your job: what you do day in and day out, the different kinds of situations you handle, the fires you put out, the problems you solve, and the initiatives you help to create. Consider the HR areas you are already familiar with because of your work: risk management, recruitment, workforce development, compensation plans, and more—all content included in the SHRM BASK. Review the SHRM BASK to highlight your areas of strength and the areas you need to develop.

Start Early!

Wouldn't it be nice to have unlimited time to prepare for the certification exam? "Sure," you think, "but I'm already so busy. How am I going to find the time to study?" The key is to start early and use the information provided here to create a plan that fits in with your life. A plan that integrates work and life can help you achieve success.

Decide the date you want to take the exam, make your appointment, commit to that date, and work backward to identify when you should start studying.

QUICK TIP

SHRM preparation programs, like the SHRM Learning System, offer custom study plans based on your experience. Your results are based on your initial pre-test results, and creates a tailored study plan to work backward from your desired exam date.

Creating time to study in a busy schedule is one reason why it's important to get started well ahead of your exam date. According to SHRM statistics, most people who achieve the highest pass rate invest between 81 and 120 hours studying. The average certification candidate spends at least 80 hours preparing for the test, and most people start studying at least three to four months ahead of time. Approximately 10 percent to 15 percent of that time is spent identifying areas where focused study is most needed to master the HR content that may appear on the exam.

However, everyone is different. How much time you will need depends partly on how much you already know through your education and experience and partly on how you prefer to learn. The strategies in this section can help you make the best use of your study time so you will be well prepared and full of confidence on test day.

 CHECK YOURSELF

Which statement most accurately describes your feelings about studying?

❑ I love learning, and I look forward to studying.

❑ I am good at managing my study time.

❑ I find studying a chore and must force myself to do it.

Chapter 4

Learn How You Learn Best

Always bear in mind that your own resolution to succeed is more important than any other.

—Abraham Lincoln

We're not all the same when it comes to learning. We receive and process information differently, and we like to learn in different ways.

Some people learn best by reading, taking notes by hand, and explaining the concepts to someone else. Others grasp new information and concepts more easily when the content is presented in visual form via charts, graphs, slides, and videos.

Understanding your learning preferences, or styles, will help you decide how best to study for success on the exam.

✓ CHECK YOURSELF

How do you think you learn best? Mark all that apply.

❑ Read the material.

❑ Hear someone explain the material.

❑ See the material presented in videos and charts.

❑ Discuss the material with other people.

❑ Explain the concepts to someone else.

❑ Take written notes on the material.

❑ Test the concepts in a real or realistic situation.

❑ Use the concepts to analyze situations and solve problems.

❑ Other:

Four Primary Learning Styles

In 1982, management experts Peter Honey and Alan Mumford published a learning styles questionnaire based on psychologist David Kolb's learning style model. Honey and Mumford identified four primary types of learners: activists, reflectors, theorists, and pragmatists. No one is entirely one type or another, but most people prefer one or two of the four styles.

Activists (Doers)

If you're an activist, you have an open-minded approach to learning and enjoy experimenting, exploring, and discovering. Anxious to practice what you learn and apply it to real-world situations, you might become impatient with lengthy discussions and explanations. Some activists might have a tendency to be disorganized and to procrastinate.

Reflectors (Reviewers or Observers)

Reflectors prefer to learn by watching or listening. If you're a reflector, you like to take your time, collect data, and examine experiences or concepts from a number of different perspectives before coming to conclusions. You might have a tendency to dislike pressure and tight deadlines.

Theorists (Thinkers)

If facts, models, concepts, and systems help you engage in the learning process, you might be described as a theorist. You like to think things through, analyze what you are learning, and understand the underlying theory. You might also tend to be more organized than other types of learners.

Pragmatists (Planners)

You might describe yourself as a pragmatist if you enjoy solving problems and sometimes become impatient with too much theory and lengthy discussions. When you learn, you want to know how the concepts apply in the real world.

Honey and Mumford: Four Learning Styles

- Activists (Doers)
- Reflectors (Reviewers or Observers)
- Theorists (Thinkers)
- Pragmatists (Planners)

ONLINE
Learn More about Honey and Mumford's Four Learning Styles

Learn more: https://expertprogrammanagement.com/2020/10/honey-and-mumford/

Video link: https://www.youtube.com/watch?v=-92dlFiN_p8

Three Ways to Learn

Researchers have also found that our learning styles differ in the ways in which we use our senses to receive and process information. One well-known theory, called VAK, postulates that most of us learn best when using one or two of our three primary sensory receivers: visual, auditory, or kinesthetic.

Visual Learners

If you're a visual learner, you like to have information presented through pictures, charts, diagrams, lists of key learning points, infographics, videos, and other visual media. Taking notes and making visual maps helps you remember what you hear or read. Interestingly, some visual learners can visualize pages on which certain information appears.

Auditory Learners

You know that you are primarily an auditory learner if you remember more of what you learn when you hear something than when you see it. You might prefer lectures and podcasts to reading. Reading aloud to yourself or talking to others about what you learn can help fix facts and concepts in your mind.

Kinesthetic Learners

You can be described as a kinesthetic learner if you find it hard to sit still for long periods. You need to stand up and move around often to keep from losing your concentration. Keeping study periods short and focused, taking notes by hand, and building frequent breaks into your study schedule can help you learn.

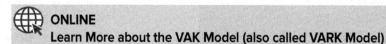 **ONLINE**
Learn More about the VAK Model (also called VARK Model)

https://vark-learn.com/introduction-to-vark/the-vark-modalities/

Cognitive Ability and Studying for Different Levels of Questions

In Chapter 2, we discussed the differences between recall, understanding, problem-solving, and critical-evaluation knowledge items—the four levels in the depth of knowledge framework. A savvy test taker studies for a SHRM certification exam by preparing for questions at varying depths of knowledge using a variety of approaches.

Reading textbooks and studying vocabulary on flash cards can be helpful techniques—not only for answering recall questions that involve definitions, but also for higher-level questions about the defined term. Test takers should be aware, however, that on a problem-solving question involving a certain term, for example, while knowing the definition of the term will help one understand what is being asked, knowing only the definition probably will not be enough to answer the question correctly.

Test takers can prepare for questions at higher cognitive levels by reading case studies, engaging in role-playing, and discussing best practices with a study group. These study techniques help one explore the benefits and consequences of actions, think about the most effective ways to solve real-life problems, and predict outcomes to guide organizations in making good decisions based on the best practices in the SHRM BASK.

SHRM Learning System

SHRM research shows that test takers who prepare for the SHRM-CP and SHRM-SCP exams using the SHRM BASK in conjunction with the SHRM Learning System pass the exams at a higher rate than those who study using neither the SHRM BASK nor the SHRM Learning System. The SHRM Learning System offers a variety of formats and tools to help you prepare for the SHRM-CP or SHRM-SCP certification exam. Approximately three-quarters of certification candidates use the Learning System to prepare for the SHRM certification exam.

SHRM has designed several learning options to suit different learning styles, schedules, group sizes, and locations. In addition to live and virtual classroom options, the Learning System is available in a fully online format. Real-life situations that require decision-making skills are incorporated into the online learning modules in addition to study tools to help you better understand, apply, and engage with behavioral competencies and HR knowledge.

HR is a profession of *doing*. HR professionals create new strategies, negotiate salaries, communicate plans, and coach managers and employees. They roll out programs to increase employee engagement, boost inclusion, and reduce organizational risk.

When HR professionals prepare for their SHRM certification exams, however, they tend to use *visual* and *auditory* modes of learning. According to SHRM data, one of the most popular ways to study for SHRM certification is to read through the SHRM BASK. Other common approaches include reading the materials provided in the SHRM Learning System, reading while flipping through flash cards or taking practice tests, and listening during prep classes or study groups. While these methods are certainly helpful, they prioritize visual and auditory learning modes and miss out on the enormous benefits of kinesthetic learning.

Adding elements of kinesthetic learning to your certification study plan can be particularly useful for improving performance on situational judgment items.

The first step is to decide where to apply this learning style. In Part 2 of this book, you'll learn how to use the SHRM BASK to identify your strengths and areas for opportunity and put together a study plan. When you are creating your study plan, identify one or two areas that you want to explore further using kinesthetic learning.

The second step is to find specific ways to incorporate kinesthetic learning into your study plan for the areas you identified. Here are a few ideas to get you started:

- **Get on-the-job training.** Ask your manager about opportunities to learn by doing, such as shadowing a colleague on a project, joining a committee to address and solve an organizational problem, or cross-training on a process or system.

- **Seek out stretch projects**. Let your manager know you are interested in receiving a stretch assignment in one or more of the areas you identified. If possible, suggest a specific project that aligns with your goals and also supports the need of the organization.

- **Enact role-play scenarios**. Ask a colleague or mentor to act out realistic HR scenarios with you. Don't limit yourself to negative situations in which you resolve conflicts or address employee complaints—go for positive situations in which you demonstrate leadership and decision-making skills, too. For instance, you could present the business case for a new human resources information system (HRIS) to an executive team or recommend actions to take based on the results of a training evaluation. Debrief with your colleague or mentor after each scenario, discussing what you did well, as well as other ways to approach such a situation in the future.

- **Gain off-the-job experience.** Use volunteer opportunities to gain experience in areas of HR that are outside of your expertise. Try offering ad-hoc HR support, or even just one-time advice, to a nonprofit organization, small business, or family member in need. Because you aren't being paid, you might feel less pressure and have more room for trial and error.

Table 4.1 shows all the formats, so you can choose those that best fit your learning styles and preferences.

Table 4.1. SHRM Learning System Formats

Instructor-Led Preparation			
EDUCATION PARTNER PROGRAMS	**CERTIFICATION PREP SEMINARS**	**SELF-STUDY PROGRAM**	**ORGANIZATIONAL TRAINING AND DEVELOPMENT**
Learn from an expert HR instructor in an engaging online or in-person classroom setting, alongside a group of fellow HR professionals, all from a local, trusted training provider.	A virtual or in-person classroom environment with interactive and comprehensive discussions, activities, and preparation techniques from a SHRM-certified, expert instructor.	Study with our learning tools, where and how you want. Optimize your time by determining your current knowledge gaps, then following your customized study path.	Customized staff training at your location, virtually, or hybrid— ensuring your team speaks the same HR language and is prepared to tackle any challenge thrown their way
Ideal for *those who prefer a structured learning environment.*	**Ideal for** *those who prefer a structured learning environment.*	**Ideal for** *those who prefer to learn on their own schedule.*	**Ideal for** *organizations that are looking for a flexible education option.*

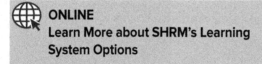

**ONLINE
Learn More about SHRM's Learning System Options**

https://www.shrm.org/credentials/certification/exam-preparation

The SHRM Learning System Is Not the SHRM Exams—and Vice Versa

You may be asking yourself, how do the SHRM BASK, SHRM Learning System, and the SHRM exams connect? The SHRM BASK is the foundation for the SHRM-CP and SHRM-SCP exams. Therefore, when test questions are created for the exams, exam writers use the SHRM BASK as their framework for questions.

The SHRM Learning System is not intended to be a replica of the exams, nor do the exams test how well you memorized the content in the SHRM Learning

System. The SHRM-CP and SHRM-SCP exams test your comprehension of the SHRM BASK, which is the foundation for the exams.

With this in mind, we highly recommend starting your study journey with the SHRM BASK and then using the SHRM Learning System to more deeply study the content in the SHRM BASK. Highlight BASK content areas that you need to study further then use the SHRM Learning System to master your knowledge of that content. You can review new content and brush up on familiar content that benefits your daily HR practice.

Why do we recommend this approach? The SHRM Learning System provides deeper learning content on content topics in the SHRM BASK that may be tested through questions on the exam. It is designed to provide training content on all areas that are covered by the certification exams (i.e., the SHRM BASK). It also provides you with opportunities to answer practice questions that are written to the same specifications as those found in the exams. Indeed, the pretest and the timed practice exam, which we designed to be taken toward the end of your study cycle, are both composed of recently administered but now retired exam questions.

These provide a realistic preview within the SHRM Learning System content, structure, and format of test questions. The SHRM Learning System study materials are intended to aid your understanding of the SHRM competencies, help you think in terms of real-life scenarios, and develop your situational judgment. Examinees are encouraged to focus not on the wording of each scenario but on the link between the competencies, sub-competencies, and proficiency indicators contained in the SHRM BASK. Focus on their practical applications by using the SHRM Learning System examples and practice questions.

Updates to the SHRM BASK, which were based on the research findings of a validation survey, led to changes effective in 2022 for both the exams and the SHRM Learning System. SHRM is committed to maintaining the relevance of the SHRM-CP and SHRM-SCP credentials, and we are committed to reviewing the content of the SHRM BASK every three to five years.

SHRM Certification Professional Development Grant

HR professionals and students are encouraged to apply for SHRM Foundation Professional Development Grants. Recipients of the grant award receive one SHRM-CP or SHRM-SCP exam, as well as access to SHRM's online Learning System. For additional information, visit https://www.shrm.org/foundation/scholarships-grants-awards/grants.

Chapter 5

Use Proven Study Strategies

Success is never accidental.

—Jack Dorsey

For some of you, it has likely been a while since you've had to study for an important exam. To prepare for the certification exam, you need to get back into study mode. The strategies in this chapter can make the difference between just studying and studying in a way that will pay off on exam day.

Keep a Positive Mindset

Imagine that two actors are preparing for the role of a lifetime. The actors are similar in terms of experience and skills. Which of them has the best chance of ending up with an award-winning performance?

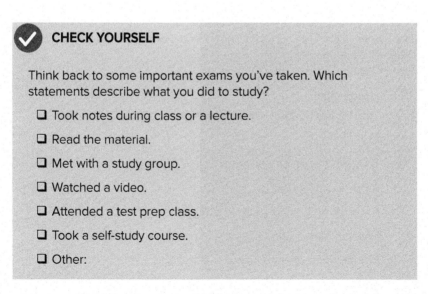

CHECK YOURSELF

Think back to some important exams you've taken. Which statements describe what you did to study?

- ❑ Took notes during class or a lecture.
- ❑ Read the material.
- ❑ Met with a study group.
- ❑ Watched a video.
- ❑ Attended a test prep class.
- ❑ Took a self-study course.
- ❑ Other:

Actor #1 worries that he isn't ready. Maybe, he thinks, he was cast in the role by mistake. Maybe he's just not good enough, and in time, everyone will notice and wish they had cast someone else.

Actor #2 firmly believes that this role is perfect for her. It will be a lot of work, she thinks, but she can't wait to get started, and she knows she will deliver a stunning performance.

There is a big difference between these two actors. It's their attitude.

Actor #1 approaches the role thinking, "I can't do this." With that attitude, chances are that he won't deliver more than a mediocre performance, if that.

Actor #2 has a very different mindset. Trusting her experience and skills, she thinks, "I *can* do this, and I can do it very well!" Her positive mindset sets her up for success as she begins the long and difficult process of learning the script and rehearsing for the role.

In terms of attitude, preparing for a certification exam is not unlike learning an acting role: if you don't believe you can pass, you set yourself up for failure. Negative thoughts like, "I can't do this" and "Other people are much better than I am" make it hard to study and to remember what you've learned on exam day.

Please do not do this to yourself. Put aside negative thinking and approach exam day with a positive mindset based on ample preparation before test day. If you approach test preparation with trust in your experience and skills and the belief that you can do well, chances are that you will. You'll find it easier to put in the work to learn the material, cope with the frustrations that learning often involves, and step out of the wings on exam day prepared to deliver the performance of your life!

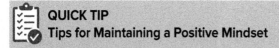

QUICK TIP
Tips for Maintaining a Positive Mindset

- Trust your experience and skills.
- Think "I can" instead of "I can't."
- Avoid comparing yourself to others.
- See the learning process as an opportunity, not a chore.
- Commit yourself to the study process and make it a top priority.

Learn Actively, Not Passively

Let's go back to the example of the actors. Actor #2 is approaching the preparation process with a positive mindset. But what if all she does to prepare is read the script and try to memorize the lines silently to herself? It's a good bet that she won't do a very good job. In fact, she's likely to forget many of the lines when she steps on the stage.

That's why actors prepare by reading their lines aloud, thinking about how their characters react to different situations, and rehearsing the scenes over and over again. In other words, the actors learn actively, not passively.

Learning experts know that passive learning, such as reading and rereading, highlighting, rote memorization, listening to lectures, and watching videos isn't enough for learners to be able to retain everything. Like the actors, being able to retain the material and then to recall it when needed requires active learning. That means doing something *with* the material to *interact* with the material.

To learn actively

» Read to remember;

» Look up unclear words and phrases;

» Develop outlines of the key facts and concepts;

» Use flash cards to help learn key terminology and facts;

» Discuss the material with other learners; and

» Explain and teach the material to others.

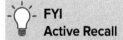 **FYI**
Active Recall

The process of learning in a way that helps you remember the information is sometimes called "active recall." It is based on the principle that in order to learn and remember the material, you need to stimulate your brain to recall it from your long-term memory when you need it—for example, when you're taking an exam.

Read to Remember

Reading is an essential part of studying. But unless you have a photographic memory, you probably forget all or most of what you read by the time you get back from a coffee break. To study effectively, you have to be able to remember what you read. There are a variety of ways to do that.

Skim What You're About to Read

Before you dive into reading a chapter or a section of the material, skim it. Don't try to understand or retain anything at this point—the purpose is to get an overview or a preview of the contents. Notice headings, text that is in boldface or italic type, and bulleted and numbered lists. Anything that is highlighted or stands out gives you clues to the content.

Take Smart Notes

Note-taking is a time-honored study tool. Taking notes helps you stay focused and engaged in the material, think critically about what you read, draw conclusions, and identify main ideas. But smart note-taking is more than dutifully copying from the text. The way you take notes should help you learn.

Here are some smart note-taking strategies to try:

» Read a short section—a couple of paragraphs, up to a page. Without looking back at the text, make notes from what you remember, trying to capture the main points in your own words. Then read the section again and fill in any important details you may have missed.

» Annotate the text. If you're reading something in print or using an electronic version that allows annotations, then you can underline, circle, add your own comments, or highlight key words and phrases.

» Look up unfamiliar words. It's very important to understand the terminology that you will find on the test. As you read, look up any words or acronyms you don't fully understand. Note the definition on the page and keep a separate list of terminology you need to study. Use the acronym list and glossary in the appendices of this book and in the SHRM BASK to review the meaning of key terms and concepts.

» Stop from time to time and think about what you're reading. Is the concept new to you, or are you already familiar with it from your own experience? In what ways might it be used or applied in the real world or on the exam? Remember that the SJIs on the exam are based on real workplace incidents encountered by HR professionals—the kinds of incidents you regularly have to handle at work. Consider how the situation presented in the scenario reflects a situation you've already experienced in your job. Then think about the decisions you made in those situations or which problems you solved by managing through a situation.

» Write summaries. Writing a summary in your own words helps you focus on the most important information facts and concepts.

» Create a visual map. Also known as a mind map, a visual map is a flowchart or diagram of your notes. One way to do it is to place the main topic in the center of the page, with the subtopics and supporting details branching off (Figure 5.1).

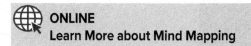

ONLINE
Learn More about Mind Mapping

"Mind Mapping," Student Services Information Desk, The University of Sheffield, https://www.sheffield.ac.uk/academic-skills/study-skills-online/mind-mapping

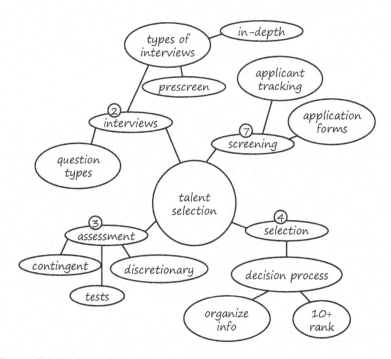

Figure 5.1. Mind Map Example

> **QUICK TIP**
> **Your Experience: The Foundation**
>
> You don't start from zero when you begin to prepare for the SHRM certification exam. You either have been working in the HR field (perhaps for many years!) or you are interested in a career in HR, so you likely already know some of the facts and concepts that will be on the test. Keep your own experience in mind as you study by thinking about the content you're learning and how it relates to your own experience.
>
> Please give yourself credit for all you have learned and all the experiences you have had over the course of your HR career. You already know and have experienced a lot—and you should not overlook that fact.

Use Flash Cards

If you've ever learned a new language, you know that flash cards can be a useful learning tool. Flash cards with key questions on the front and the answers on the back are terrific study tools that help you learn and see how well you are retaining what you learn. When you look at the first side of the card, you either know what's on the other side or you don't. If you don't, you'll know to keep working on that fact, term, acronym, or concept. However, please note that flash cards will likely not be the best way to learn behavioral competencies or to learn to effectively answer situational judgment items (Figure 5.2). Those questions are based on your experience.

job enlargement	**process of broadening a job's scope by adding different tasks to the job.**

Figure 5.2. Flash Cards Example

The Leitner System

Austrian science writer Sebastian Leitner developed the Leitner system for using flash cards to improve his own ability to retain what he learned. The powerful technique to help you recall what you study is called *spaced repetition*.

Leitner set up a box with several compartments. He put new flash cards in the first compartment and used them every day to test his recall of what he was learning. When he answered a question correctly, he moved the flash card to a second compartment.

Every two days, he tried again to answer the questions on the flash cards in the second compartment. The ones he got right moved to a third compartment, and the ones he got wrong moved back to the first compartment.

Several days later, he tried to answer the questions on the cards in the third compartment. This time, the ones he got wrong moved back to the first compartment and the ones he got right moved to a fourth compartment. As cards moved into higher compartments, he tested himself on those topics less and less frequently, focusing instead on the topics he had difficulty recalling

Tips for Using Flash Cards

» Set up a box like Leitner's, with separate compartments, or create your own variation with single boxes or rubber bands that separate the levels of cards into packs.

» If you use the SHRM Learning System to help you prepare for the exam, you have access to online, interactive flashcards and the option to download and print. Use your mobile phone to access the digital flashcards or carry your printed flashcards anywhere you go so you can test yourself while you're standing in line, waiting for an appointment, or have a few minutes of spare time. It will surprise you how much studying you do during those dead times.

 ONLINE

Put the words "create flash cards" into a web browser, and you'll find a variety of low-cost tools for making your own.

Be the Teacher

A great way to see how well you understand and can recall what you're learning is to explain or teach it to others. Trying to convey facts and information to someone who knows little or nothing about the subject helps you quickly discover what you know well and what you need to work on.

The Feynman Technique

When he was a student at Princeton, physicist Richard Feynman developed an active recall system that relied heavily on the idea of teaching what he was learning to a child.

> "A co-worker and I participated in a group training program through the local SHRM chapter. We both purchased the learning materials and combined [them] with the group sessions [which] provided additional support and interaction that more fully prepared us for the exam."

The idea is that teaching a child forces you to break down what you're learning and translate it into clear, simple language. You can do that only if you truly understand it. The process helps you remember what you've already learned and discover the gaps in your learning.

You don't have to have a child around to practice this technique. Your student can be anyone who is unfamiliar with the subject. Plan a lesson to teach something you're learning to that person. When you use your notes to teach, you'll quickly discover how well you actually know the material.

ONLINE
Learn More about Active Recall, the Leitner System, and the Feynman Technique

"What is Active Recall? How to Use It to Ace Your Exams," *Brainscape*, https://www.brainscape.com/academy/active-recall-definition-studying/

Robert Harris, "Learning Strategy 10: The Leitner Flash Card System," February 27, 2014, https://www.virtualsalt.com/learning-strategy-10-the-leitner-flash-card-system/

"Learning From the Feynman Technique," *Evernote* (blog), July 21, 2017, https://medium.com/taking-note/learning-from-the-feynman-technique-5373014ad230

Study with Others

✓ **CHECK YOURSELF**

Have you ever worked with a group to help you learn or to prepare for an exam? In what ways was the group helpful?

_____

_____

_____

_____

_____

_____

_____

_____

_____

_____

Studying with other learners can be a vital part of the learning process. In fact, researchers from other testing programs have found that people who study together in groups often succeed at a higher rate than students who study alone. Study group members help one another understand the material, review what they are learning, and identify gaps in their learning. They share resources and help one another build confidence as they prepare for the exam.

Study group members typically meet face-to-face, usually once or twice a week. But if there are not enough test takers for a face-to-face group in your area, you can find or form a virtual group with other HR professionals who are preparing for the same test. Your local SHRM chapter can help.

 **ONLINE**
Find Your Local SHRM Chapter

https://www.shrm.org/community/chapters

How Study Groups Can Help Prepare You for Answering SJIs

Study groups are particularly helpful to prepare for answering SJIs when group members work together to explore critical incidents in their own workplaces.

Here's how: Ask each member to present a critical incident that happened recently at work. For each incident, the group discusses.

» What happened, what HR issues (such as compensation or ethics) were involved, and what challenges the incident posed.

» What to consider when addressing the challenges, such as who was involved, time pressures, possible results of action or inaction, and so forth.

» What best practice would have been in the given situation. (Hint: Use the proficiency indicators in the SHRM BASK to help determine this!)

Tips for Making the Most of Study Group Time

» Choose group members who are studying for the same test, either the SHRM-CP or SHRM-SCP.

» Keep the group to a manageable size—three to five people is ideal.

» Have a specific agenda for each meeting that shows the topics to be covered, time allotted for each topic, who will bring what, and so on.

» Use assignments to encourage everyone to participate. For example, ask everyone to come prepared to explain or teach one topic to the others.

» Limit socializing to the first and last five minutes of the meeting. Another option is to discuss study pain points for the first five minutes and study pain points resolutions for the last five minutes.

» Schedule regular meetings, and try to schedule them for the same days and times.

» Choose a place that is free of distractions and where you are unlikely to be interrupted.

» For each meeting, choose a moderator who will step in as needed to keep the meeting on track and make sure everyone has a chance to participate. If needed, set time limits to keep one person from dominating discussions.

» Close each meeting by having everyone mention something they learned.

» Before the end of each meeting, set up the agenda and choose the moderator for the next one.

» Between meetings, use email or text to ask the other members questions that come up as you study.

» After each meeting, list the topics you do not fully know and understand and adjust your study plan as needed.

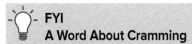

FYI
A Word About Cramming

Cramming is the practice of working furiously to try to absorb a lot of information in a short amount of time, usually just before a test. We've all done it when we have to take a test for which we haven't really studied. But researchers have found that learners are seldom able recall much information after cramming. Cramming just before a test can be a helpful way to review the material, but it takes dedicated study to learn.

Many SHRM certification exam test takers have reported that they chose to cram instead of study—and it did not work. In fact, it turned out to be a very ineffective strategy. Do not cram for a SHRM exam. Study.

Other Study Tips

» **Learn from former test takers**. People who have already earned their SHRM-CP or SHRM-SCP certification can be a great source of tips and advice. Because they have already gone through the process, they have the advantage of hindsight: what worked and what they wish they had done differently.

» **Take an exam preparation course.** Explore the entire SHRM BASK with the guidance of an expert, SHRM-certified instructor while collaborating with other HR pros like you. You'll also get access to the premier learning solution: the SHRM Learning System which includes online reading modules, study tools, practice exams, and more to help prepare you for success on exam day.

» **Pace yourself and take study breaks.** Studying takes an enormous amount of concentration and energy. Schedule breaks during your study sessions. Stand up and stretch, walk around, or get a snack.

But avoid the temptation to distract yourself by checking your phone or email!

» **Make time for yourself.** Taking time away from study—from even thinking about the exam—not only helps you feel better, it keeps you from suffering information overload. Make time for activities that you enjoy and that help you stay healthy. Relax with family and friends. Go for long walks or a run. Go to the gym, take a yoga class, or get a massage. Refreshing yourself helps you feel more relaxed, which in turn helps you concentrate on what you need to learn.

QUICK TIP
Study Best Practices

- Learn actively, not passively.
- Read to remember.
- Use flash cards to learn facts and terminology.
- Be the teacher.
- Study with others.
- Share experiences when preparing for SJIs.
- Learn from former test takers.
- Take an exam preparation course.
- Pace yourself and take study breaks.
- Make time for yourself.

ONLINE
Learn More about Using Flash Cards and Taking Notes

Thomas Frank, "How to Study Effectively with Flash Cards," July 26, 2016, YouTube video, 8:43, https://www.youtube.com/watch?v=mzCEJVtED0U

Jennifer Gonzalez, "Note-taking: A Research Roundup," *Cult of Pedagogy* (blog), September 9, 2018, https://www.cultofpedagogy.com/note-taking/

Crash Course, "Taking Notes: Crash Course Study Skills #1," August 8, 2017, YouTube video, 8:50, https://www.youtube.com/watch?v=E7CwqNHn_Ns

Chapter 6

Where and When You Study Matters

Education is the passport to the future, for tomorrow belongs to those who prepare for it today.

—Malcolm X

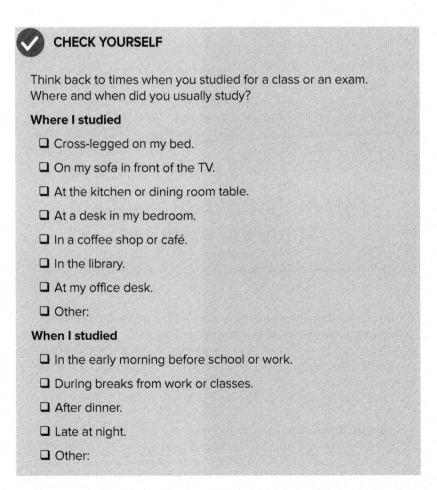

CHECK YOURSELF

Think back to times when you studied for a class or an exam. Where and when did you usually study?

Where I studied

❑ Cross-legged on my bed.

❑ On my sofa in front of the TV.

❑ At the kitchen or dining room table.

❑ At a desk in my bedroom.

❑ In a coffee shop or café.

❑ In the library.

❑ At my office desk.

❑ Other:

When I studied

❑ In the early morning before school or work.

❑ During breaks from work or classes.

❑ After dinner.

❑ Late at night.

❑ Other:

Walk into any coffee shop anywhere in the world, and you will likely see people hard at work on laptops or with books and notepads next to their coffee cups. Some people concentrate well when other people are nearby, in front of the TV, late at night, or in brief periods between other activities. But most of us find it easier to focus on work or study in a place that is quiet, comfortable, and free of distractions; when we block out specific times for study; and when we are rested and alert.

If you are getting back into the studying game after a multi-year hiatus, you may be tempted to revert to studying techniques that—for better or worse—served you in the past. Keep in mind, that studying was likely accompanied by auditory instruction from a teacher, presenter, or instructor. Unless you engage in one of SHRM's in-person or virtual instructor-led programs focusing on the Learning System, you may need to adjust your approach.

> **QUICK TIP**
> **Studying While Traveling**
>
> If your job involves a lot of travel, you might have to study while on the road, so you'll have to find a quiet place in which you can concentrate. Your hotel room will be private and, hopefully, quiet with few distractions. Most hotels also have quiet public spaces such as conference rooms or quiet lobby areas. If not, ask the hotel desk where to find a library.

Tips for Setting Up the Right Study Environment

» **Study in the same place regularly.** Designate a place for yourself where you expect to study regularly.

» **Unless you study best when others are around, choose a quiet place where you are unlikely to be disturbed or distracted**—not a busy café, the company cafeteria, your desk during work hours, the sofa in front of the TV, or the kitchen table while your kids are awake. If you can't set up a study place at home, your local library probably has a spot where you can work, or maybe your company has a private room you can use in the off hours.

» **Minimize distractions and interruptions.** Turn off your phone (or leave it somewhere else). If you use the computer to study, turn off email notifications. If you're studying in the office or at home while family members or roommates are around, ask everyone not to disturb you. If necessary, put a sign on the door that says, "Working—please don't disturb me!"

» **Make sure you have everything you need.** Set up your study space so you don't have to interrupt yourself to get water to stay hydrated, snacks for extra energy, or coffee if needed.

» **Make yourself comfortable.** You'll need good light, a comfortable chair, enough room to spread out learning materials, pens or pencils, writing tablets, a laptop if you'll be using it, and so on. Arrange all those things ahead of time so you can focus on learning.

» **Keep a regular study schedule.** Set aside certain hours of each day for study just as you do for meals, sleep, and exercise. Choose a time of day when you'll feel rested and alert. If you work full-time, decide whether you're at your best early in the morning or in the evening. If you have free time during the day, decide whether you're at your best in the mornings or the afternoons. Also consider the times of day when you are least likely to be interrupted.

QUICK TIP
How to Decide Where and When to Study

- Study in the same place regularly.

- Study where you are unlikely to be disturbed or distracted.

- Minimize distractions and interruptions.

- Make sure you have everything you need.

- Make yourself comfortable.

- Keep a regular study schedule.

DIRECTIONS
Where and When Will You Study?

Where I will study:

_____

_____

When I will study:

_____

_____

Chapter 7

Create a SMART Study Plan

Success isn't overnight. It's when every day you get a little better than the day before. It all adds up.

—Dwayne Johnson

Imagine this: you have two weeks of vacation coming up. You've decided to use that time to travel somewhere you've never been. You're very excited about taking this trip, and you want it to be perfect!

But perfect doesn't just happen. Great trips require careful planning. You need to decide where you will go, how you will get there, where you will stay, what you will see and do, what to pack, and more. With careful planning, you can leave for your trip relaxed and confident that you will have a wonderful time.

Perfect doesn't just happen when you prepare for an exam, either. It takes a thoughtfully created study plan for you to be relaxed and confident on test day. Your study plan will help you

» Make the best use of the time you have available to study,

» Set priorities so you focus on the right work at the right time, and

» Avoid procrastinating and keep yourself on track.

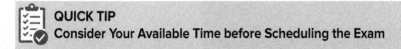

QUICK TIP
Consider Your Available Time before Scheduling the Exam

To set yourself up for success, consider how much study time you'll have available *before* you schedule the exam. It's better to wait for the next exam window than to try cramming too much study into too little time.

What Your Study Plan Should Include

A well-designed study plan includes the following:

» Your study **schedule**: a calendar showing the dates and times you have set aside for study, including time for study group meetings.

» Your **goal** for each study session. For example, you might want to be able to list the "three most important . . ." or "describe the best way to . . ." All of these and others you create as part of your plan will prepare you to respond to questions on the SHRM exam.

» The **content** you will cover during each study session to achieve your goal for that session.

» The **checkpoints** at which you will assess your progress. This includes when you will take practice tests and when you will assess if you need to adjust your study plan to fill in your learning gaps

A thorough study plan doesn't only include how you will learn the HR behaviors and knowledge you need for the exam—it also includes familiarizing yourself with how the exam is displayed in the testing platform. For instance, for SJIs, you will first see a screen with the scenario by itself, followed by one screen per question, which also includes the scenario. This format allows you a continued view of all pertinent information at the same time (e.g., scenario, question, and response options all on the same page) and allows you to refer back to the scenario if needed. Being aware of and comfortable with the functionality of the exam platform can help save you time on exam day and reduce test anxiety. (For more on test anxiety, see Part 3.)

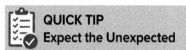

QUICK TIP
Expect the Unexpected

Things happen to throw the most carefully crafted study plan off track. You or a family member might get sick. There might be a crisis at work. It might take longer than you thought to learn a particular topic. Leave extra time in your study schedule so you can catch up if you get behind.

How to Create Your Study Plan

As we said earlier, the SHRM BASK is basis for the blueprint for both the SHRM-CP and SHRM-SCP exams. The better you familiarize yourself with this document, the better you will understand how the exam is structured.

All the questions on the exam are based on the topics covered in the SHRM BASK. Thus, the purpose of studying is to close the gaps between what you already know from your experience in the HR field and what you need to know to become certified. That's why your study plan should start with identifying those gaps. Once you know what you need to learn, you can decide how to focus your study time and set up a workable study schedule. Step one in creating your study plan is to review and note areas for further study in the SHRM BASK. Suggestions for doing this appear in the next section.

Identify Your Strengths and Areas for Focus

Start by reading through the SHRM BASK to become familiar with the breadth and depth of content on the exam, as well as the format of the SHRM BASK.

Once you are familiar with the SHRM BASK in general, review one behavioral competency or functional area at a time. Read the definition, the sub-competencies (for behavioral competencies), the key concepts, and the proficiency indicators for the exam level you selected. Note the topics and terminology that you are already familiar with from your HR experience and those that are new to you or presented in a new way.

One effective way to do this is to review the SHRM BASK using highlighter pens (either on paper or electronically). For example, you could use one color to highlight topics in the SHRM BASK where your familiarity or knowledge is limited, then use a different color to highlight topics in the SHRM BASK where you have a solid command of knowledge for the topic area.

Next, think about your level of expertise in all the areas that are outlined. For the functional areas, this will primarily be the things that you know and know how to do, such as learning and development or risk management. To think through the behavioral competencies and how they manifest themselves in your daily work, think about situations, problems, and challenges you encounter at work. Think about how the different behavioral competencies are often used in tandem to approach and resolve issues, make decisions, or solve problems and challenges. For example, communication, global mindset, and ethical practice may all be needed to resolve an issue. Similarly, business acumen, relationship management, and consultation may be combined to effectively solve a problem.

Based on your level of expertise for each behavioral competency or functional area, rate yourself on a three-point scale:

» **Study most**
   These are areas where you have little to no experience. If you primarily support employee relations and employee engagement, you may need to study most in areas such as talent acquisition or global mindset because you have little to no hands-on experience in this area.

» **Study some**
   These are areas where you have some experience, but you're not an expert. This could apply if you are a generalist with experience across many (or even most) competencies; you might have a surface-level knowledge of the competency, but you need to spend some time studying to better understand that competency outside of just your role or organization. If you used to work in a specific area but now perform a different set of job duties, this might apply too.

» **Review**
   These are the areas where you have the most experience. When you create your study plan, you don't want to spend too much time on these areas. Instead, you'll devote that time to studying the areas where you have more to learn.

When you are finished rating yourself, you should have twenty-three discrete ratings, one for each behavioral competency and functional area. Review your ratings and make notes about the terms, facts, and concepts that you need to learn or know more about so you can include them in your study plan.

It is important to review but not overstudy areas where your knowledge and familiarity with the content is already at a command-and-control level. Instead, focus your study efforts to improve your knowledge on the content with which you are least familiar. This means you should spend the majority of your study time on your study most areas, some time on your study some areas, and only a small amount of time on your review areas.

Once you complete your self-assessment, group together the items on your checklist that you can study together. Think about these groups as study blocks. As you sort items into groups, list the related terms and acronyms for each. Once you identify your study blocks, you'll have the outline for your study plan. Recall the SHRM Learning System offers the ability to create a study plan, identifying your areas of strengths and weaknesses based on your pre-test score.

Set Up a Realistic Study Schedule

Your study schedule is a detailed calendar that shows when you will study specific items on your checklist (Figure 7.1). Here's how to create that schedule:

1. **How much time do I need?**
   Figure out how many hours you will need to cover everything on your study checklist. Consider factors such as the extent of your HR experience and how quickly you tend to learn.

2. **How much time do I have?**
   Determine how much of your time is already committed elsewhere. Consider the time you need for family, work, exercise, personal care, and social activities, along with down time and time for the unexpected, such as illness or a heavier-than-usual workload.

3. **What will each week look like?**
   Decide how many hours of study time you will have available each week before the exam. If you plan to form or join a study group or take an exam prep course, identify how many hours each week you will need for those activities. Then divide the remaining time into study sessions.

4. **What are my study goals?**
   Determine a specific, achievable goal for each study session and identify the content you will study so you can achieve that goal. Keep in mind that you'll need more study time for some content areas, and build time into your schedule for practice tests so that you can track your progress.

5. **What's my schedule?**
   Develop a realistic study schedule that shows your study sessions by date and time, the goal for each session, and the content you'll focus on during that session.

6. **What should my study calendar include?**
   Create a week-by-week calendar that includes your scheduled activities for each day during your study period. Include time for

   > Family and friends

   > Work (including your commute)

   > Scheduled appointments (doctors, dentists, etc.)

   > Exercise

   > Study sessions, study group meetings, and exam prep courses (if any)

7. **Did I miss anything?**
Step back and review your calendar. How realistic is it? Did you leave time for meals and personal care, as well as some down time so you can rest and relax? Did you leave buffer time in case something unexpected arises?

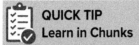

QUICK TIP
Learn in Chunks

Be careful not to try learning too much during any one session. Researchers have found that studying small chunks of content and repeatedly testing yourself on what you've learned helps you remember the information so you can recall it on exam day.

ONLINE

Kendra Cherry, "How the Chunking Technique Can Help Improve Your Memory," *Very Well Mind*, updated July 12, 2020, https://www.verywellmind.com/chunking-how-can-this-technique-improve-your-memory-2794969

My study schedule for: [week] _____
Test date: _____
Goal: Become proficient in global and cultural effectiveness

Monday	Tuesday	Wednesday	Thursday	Friday	Saturday	Sunday
7:30–9:30 p.m.	7:30–9:30 p.m.	7:30–9:30 p.m.	7:30–9:30 p.m.	No study	10:00–noon	4:00–6:30 p.m.
Read Global Mindset Competency	*Focus*: strategies to develop global mindset; list skills needed for global HR	*Focus*: culture: definition, layers, and theories	*Focus*: obstacles to cross-cultural understanding and strategies to negotiate cultural differences		Meet with study group 3:30–5:30 p.m. *Focus*: related terminology	Review and practice questions

Figure 7.1. Excerpt from Study Plan Calendar

✅ **CHECK YOURSELF**

❏ I have a goal for each study session and have identified the content to cover so I can reach that goal.

❏ I have a realistic study schedule that considers my other responsibilities, myself, and the unexpected.

❏ I study at a time of day when I am most rested, alert, and able to concentrate.

❏ I have set up a regular, comfortable place to study where I am unlikely to be disturbed or distracted.

❏ I will take steps to minimize distractions and interruptions while I am studying.

❏ I will make studying a priority.

❏ Other:

Part 3

Sharpen Your
Test-Taking Skills

*Satisfaction lies in the effort, not in the
attainment, full effort is full victory.*

—Mahatma Gandhi

There are all kinds of misconceptions about multiple-choice exams. Some believe exam writers throw in questions to lead you in the wrong direction or order the responses to provide clues about which option is correct. Some believe it's better to skip a question than make a wrong guess and that a long answer is always more likely to be right than a short answer. The list of misperceptions goes on, but all these urban legends stem from the belief that exam questions don't really ask what they seem to ask—that there's hidden meaning behind the questions and the exam writers' true intent is to trip up test takers.

None of those statements are true about the SHRM-CP and SHRM-SCP exams (see Figure P3.1). There are no trick questions, and there is no SHRM answer. You will not be given "none of the above" or "all of the above" choices. A response can be true but not necessarily right in the context of the question asked. There might be more than one effective response to questions posed about a situational judgment item based on a scenario, but only one will be best in the context presented. The order of the responses has nothing to do with whether a response is correct.

Myth	Myth Debunked
Myth #1 "Look for the SHRM answer."	**Incorrect**. Even though this advice appears in many social media discussions, it is absolutely *wrong*. Do not look for the SHRM answer. In short, there are no SHRM questions or SHRM answers because while SHRM manages the process, we DO NOT write the questions. All the items on the SHRM exams are written by SHRM-certified HR professionals using the SHRM BASK as their guide, and the questions are rigorously validated to make sure that they accurately measure your HR knowledge. So instead of relying on this urban legend, use your reasoning skills, your HR experience, and what you've learned from studying to decide which responses to select.
Myth #2 "Look for clues to the right answer to a knowledge question—often the longest or shortest answer is correct."	**Also wrong**. Each SHRM-certified HR subject matter expert must write four plausible response options of approximately the same length. They are specifically told not to write tricky questions, so don't look for clues like the length of the response. There aren't any.
Myth #3 "I've got a lot of experience, so I can wing it—I don't need to prepare."	**Not advisable**. SHRM research on the certification exams consistently shows that examinees who do not prepare for their exam pass at a much lower rate than anyone else. You need to know the subject matter, so leverage the resources you have and create a study plan to help you succeed.
Myth #4 "Situational judgment items scare me; I know I'm not going to do well on those."	**Shift your point of view**. Remember that you manage similar situations every day at work (or at least most of you do). Think about similar challenges you've encountered or problems you've solved—how did you decide which course of action to take in those situations? Think about best practices in HR. All these will help you prepare so you will feel more confident on test day.
Myth #5 "The exam automatically presents successively more difficult questions each time you answer a question correctly."	**Untrue**. Dynamic or adaptive exams present successively more difficult questions after an examinee answers the previous question correctly—but the SHRM exams are not dynamic exams. While there are standardized tests on the market that are dynamic exams (such as the GRE), the SHRM-CP and SHRM-SCP exams are not built this way and are not administered this way.

Figure P3.1. Dispelling Five Myths about the SHRM Certification Exam

Chapter 8

Practice Makes Perfect!

It does not matter how slowly you go as long as you do not stop.

—Confucius

Roger Federer wasn't born a number one tennis player, and Yo-Yo Ma didn't just pick up a cello one day and start making beautiful music. It takes lots and lots of practice to master a skill.

Test taking is also a skill that takes practice to develop.

That's why taking at least one practice test is important to become familiar with the structure of the exam, along with an overview of the topics—bridging the gap between your current knowledge and what you need to know in preparation for the exam. Practicing helps you answer the test questions more quickly and manage the testing time more effectively.

As you might have guessed, the theme of this chapter is practice! SHRM offers multiple products offering SHRM-developed practice item sets. At the end of this book, there are 50 practice item sets that combine 25 SHRM-CP and 25 SHRM-SCP questions. If you decide to use the SHRM Learning System to help you prepare for the exam, you'll have more opportunities to practice with thousands of items, including full-length, timed practice tests.

Note that the practice item sets in this book, as well as the official practice tests in the SHRM Learning System, SHRM-CP and SHRM-SCP Exam Workbooks, and other SHRM resources are created with previously used SHRM exam items. These are the most realistic items that best represent the SHRM-CP and SHRM-SCP exams both from an HR content perspective, as well as in their style and format, which you can use to kick-start your preparation for your exam.

Practice items that you find in study resources produced outside of SHRM will not accurately portray the kinds of items included on the actual SHRM exams.

QUICK TIP

Use the SHRM BASK as a guide while preparing for the SHRM-CP or SHRM-SCP exams. The SHRM BASK is the blueprint for creating both exams, which includes fourteen HR functional areas (technical expertise) and nine behavioral competencies.

How to Get the Most Out of Practice Tests

Choosing the right time to start preparing for your exam is important. Preparation is the key. There is no universal approach to exam preparation that works for all. You should begin with the end goal in mind! If you have a date scheduled to take the SHRM-CP or SHRM-SCP exam, backward planning or reverse planning may be an effective technique for creating your study plan.

The mindset behind preparing for the exam and incorporating practice tests is to overcome test anxiety and procrastination (see Chapter 10). You can apply these steps to optimize your experience using the practice tests:

1. Organize the specific areas you need to study, such as listing the SHRM BASK.

2. Categorize competencies (behavioral and technical) that you will need to focus on more based on your results from the practice test. However, it does not mean you neglect the other competencies you may have performed well on; it is a method, when put into practice, that helps you constructively focus your efforts toward a successful outcome.

3. In addition to this book, select the practice test or practice item sets that best fit your needs.

   a.   Preparing for the SHRM-CP Exam Workbook, which includes over seventy practice test items.

   b.   Preparing for the SHRM-SCP Exam Workbook, which includes over seventy practice test items.

   c.   SHRM Learning System practice questions and practice official tests.

4. Take a moment to review your performance related to the competency areas in the SHRM BASK (as mentioned in Step 2).

5. Create your study plan (see Chapter 7).

6. Commit to your study schedule.

7. Retake the practice test again and reassess your performance. Additionally, explore additional SHRM offerings like the SHRM Learning System for a comprehensive study approach.

FYI
Creating a Testing Environment

Fear of the unknown can trigger anxieties that impact performance, and overconfidence can lead to underperforming. In a 2017 TED talk, Sian Beilock said, "Whether taking a test or giving a talk, it is easy to feel at the top of our game and then perform at our worst when it matters most." But why? Beilock answers, "It turns out that rarely do we practice under the types of conditions we're actually going to perform under and as a result, when all eyes are on us, we sometimes flub our performance." From this, we can discern that how you prepare can impact your performance. Whether you are taking a practice test in the SHRM Learning System or answering retired test questions in the Preparing for the SHRM-CP Exam or Preparing for the SHRM-SCP Exam workbooks, set up your space to closely imitate how it will be on test day. Remove distractions and notify those in your space that you cannot be interrupted. Practicing taking the exam in similar conditions to those you will experience on test day will remove any anxieties felt from the new environment or time expectations—highlighting what areas you need to focus on without test anxiety influencing your performance.

To view the full TED talk, navigate to this list: https://www.ted.com/speakers/sian_leah_beilock

If you can, take the practice tests on a computer to experience the way you'll be tested in the exam room. You'll be able to answer some questions more quickly than others but pace yourself against the average time allotted per question, which is ninety-eight seconds on average. When it comes to practicing, you can take either timed or untimed practice exams with the aid of your study materials or in a closed-book way. We'll discuss the benefits of these different approaches further in the next section.

> **QUICK TIP**
> **Practice Timing the Test**
>
> When you take the SHRM exam, you'll have three hours and forty minutes to answer 134 questions. That breaks down to an average of about one and one half minutes per question (ninety-eight seconds to be exact). You'll be able to answer some questions much more quickly, leaving time for lengthier situational judgment questions, or items you find more difficult.
>
> Timing yourself when you practice will help you develop a sense of how long it takes to answer both easy and difficult questions. SHRM Learning System includes timed practice tests using previously tested SHRM-CP and SHRM-SCP exam items, respectively.

Assess Your Performance

After you take a practice exam, it's essential to assess your performance. Here are a few more tips for using practice tests effectively:

» Figure out why you incorrectly answered a question and pinpoint what you need to study. Did you get a fact or some terminology wrong? Did you not read the scenario carefully enough?

» Ask yourself, what questions was I unsure of? Where did I have to guess? Feeling uncertain about which answer to select could indicate that you don't know that topic as well as you should.

» Take as many different official SHRM practice tests as you can.

» When you take timed, closed-book tests, resist the temptation to refer to your learning materials. Put them away and take the test as if it were the real thing. Push yourself to retain information.

» Create your own practice tests honing in on areas you feel less confident in. Write questions for topics that you don't fully know or understand. Put the test aside while you study those topics. Then try to answer the questions.

» Use the practice tests to exercise your HR knowledge to reason through the longer, more complex SJI questions. See Chapter 9 for strategies.

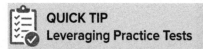

QUICK TIP
Leveraging Practice Tests

The SHRM Learning System has over 2,700 practice questions that are designed to reflect the look and feel of SHRM exam questions.

In addition, there is a practice test (based on previously used exam questions). We recommend that students opt to review both CP and SCP questions for further practice.

ONLINE

Use online practice questions to get experience answering the types of questions you'll find on the certification exam: https://pages.shrm.org/certpracticequestions

FYI
Sijia's Story: Valuing My Connection to the SHRM Certification Community

Professors and colleagues always cited SHRM as a trustworthy and resourceful HR community, so when I decided to become a certified practitioner, I chose to take the SHRM-CP exam. Now that I am a credential-holder, people from the US and other countries see those letters after my name and admire my achievement. For me, the true value of SHRM certification is finding myself in a larger community and the sense of belonging.

Preparing for the SHRM-CP exam took me back to my time in graduate school, when I was also reading, doing research, and sharing views with other students. The SHRM Body of Applied Skills and Knowledge (SHRM BASK) was a well-developed structure within which I could holistically strengthen my academic HR knowledge, as well as apply that knowledge to real-world client cases. Often during my exam prep, I found inspiring answers to client issues.

Support in My Career as a Consultant

I continue to find the SHRM competencies helpful in my work as a young professional in a big consulting firm in China. More company management teams are accepting the competency concept, which in turn (and more importantly) inspires HR practitioners to adopt the right skill sets for facing new challenges. Technical competencies are required by the job, but behavioral competencies enable HR professionals to become true business partners and create value for the organization.

The *business acumen* competency, for example, echoed recently throughout a client project involving HR transformation. My team facilitated a shift in mindset from responding to business requests to proactively thinking about business needs and providing services that deliver people-oriented value. That mindset shift was supported by my ability to understand the organization's strategy, operations, and external environments, the essence of business acumen.

With my SHRM-CP credential, I have gained the trust of clients looking for a consultant with global insights and a solid understanding of people and organizations. My proficiency in HR knowledge areas and the *global mindset* competency played a role in another recent project for a client that wanted to improve its employee experience across several geographic regions. I was able to help raise the client's awareness of the cultural and mindset differences between its regional leaders (who were mostly from the West) and local staff (who were located in countries across Asia that had quite different cultures and religions, despite being neighbors). The client was then able to place further emphasis on diversity in assessing the project's current status and in planning appropriate initiatives.

Recertification and Enriching HR Knowledge

Study never ends, even after one passes the certification exam.

I use my free time, usually while traveling to and from the office or clients' offices, to read SHRM's *HR Magazine* and newsletters and catch up with popular topics across industries. I also learn from the stories of other SHRM credential-holders to see how I might further elevate my career. At work, the SHRM website is the first resource I go to for insights and practice aids and what I recommend to colleagues and clients. The SHRM Connect online community is where HR peers discuss real issues we encounter daily, express diverse ideas, and debate possible solutions. I find the conversations inspiring, as they expose me to cases in the corporate world—a perfect supplement to my work in the consultancy world.

It was most exciting to be invited to join in SHRM-CP test-development activities and to work virtually with a diverse team. Since 2017 I have participated in several rounds of technical review, content validation, bias and cultural sensitivity review, and other important activities, which help to maintain a consistent and high standard for upcoming tests. Completing my assignments and submitting them on time are part of my commitment to HR professionalism.

When I lived in the Washington, DC, area, I saw the SHRM headquarters building in nearby Alexandria, VA, as a symbol of knowledge. Now, as a SHRM member living on the other side of the Pacific Ocean, each virtual meeting is a great opportunity for me to feel more connected to the larger community of SHRM-CP credential-holders.

—Sijia Bu, SHRM-CP

Chapter 9

Put On Your Thinking Cap

How to Reason through an Item

If opportunity doesn't knock, build a door.

—Milton Berle

The questions on SHRM's certification exams are designed to assess your expertise as an HR professional. SHRM-certified HR experts in the field write and vet each question thoroughly. There are no trick questions on the exams. However, there are strategies that can help you decide which answer to choose.

To determine which approaches are most and least effective, SHRM conducted a series of item interviews with professionals during April and May 2021. We interviewed

» Certified professionals who previously scored highly on the SHRM-CP or SHRM-SCP exam,

» Professionals who previously failed one of the SHRM exams, and

» Professionals who had never taken either SHRM certification exam.

During these interviews, a SHRM certification team member presented each professional with a series of previously used SHRM-CP and SHRM-SCP exam items. The SHRM team member carefully observed how these professionals approached each item, noted whether those strategies led to correct or incorrect answers, and looked for patterns in the results. The findings from these interviews heavily influenced the contents of this chapter to ensure you are equipped with the best strategies for passing your exam.

Effective Test-Taking Strategies

Read Carefully Before Choosing an Answer

This seemingly simple advice will go a long way. The way you read the questions and response options before answering can make a significant difference. When you simply skim instead of reading thoroughly, you might misunderstand the question or miss something important in the question—leading to an incorrect choice.

For that reason, be sure to read the entire question and all the response options carefully. For example, if a question asks for a program, make sure your answer is a program. Similarly, if the question asks for a strategy or method, make sure that your answer is also a strategy or method.

For Knowledge Items (KIs)

Read the Question First, Then *All* the Response Options

Read the question before you read the response options. Pause and ask yourself, "What is the question actually asking?" While you read, look for key words or phrases in the question that suggest steps, process, or hierarchy. Pick out key words or phrases like "first," "immediately," "most important," or "most effective." Depending on the item, all the response options may be steps, important factors, and so forth. As the test taker, select the one that correctly matches the key word or phrase in the question. If you struggle with an item, flag it to return to later. Remember to highlight key words or phrases—such as mentions of steps or hierarchy—to help jog your memory when you return to it later.

Identify Key HR Terms

While you are reading, it is also important to identify key HR terms. Successful examinees identify key HR terms and consider what they know about that topic as they read. For example, if you're reading an item about succession planning, you might think to yourself, "This company is focused on succession planning, so I know they are thinking about building their talent pipeline." If you're reading an item about performing the last step in the ADDIE model, you might think to yourself, "I know the ADDIE model. Evaluation is the last step, and it is used to assess the quality and effectiveness of the training solution."

If you encounter a term that you don't know, start by breaking it into parts to try to figure out what it might mean. This could mean looking at root words within the term or separate words in the phrase. During the item interviews, some participants weren't quite sure about the meaning of "product differentiation strategy." Those who broke the phrase down into parts were more likely to get the item correct. Here's an example of what this looks like:

"product differentiation strategy" =

"product" + "*differenti*ation" + "strategy" =

a "strategy" to make your "product" "different" or stand out in the market

For Situational Judgment Items (SJIs)

Read the Scenario First

Based on the results of the item interviews, SHRM recommends reading the entire scenario first. This is because reading the scenario gives you the context you need to fully understand an item. It can also be helpful to jot down key points using the virtual scratchpad on the Prometric testing platform or use the highlight feature as you read. A scenario may appear intimidating at first, but breaking it into digestible chunks helps you remember the relevant pieces as you read the response options.

Once you have read the scenario, then read the question and *all* of the response options. Do not stop at the first one you think might be right; there might be a better response among the other choices. Similarly, make sure to read every response option before eliminating any of them so that you fully understand the item. If you start eliminating options before you read all the options, you could eliminate them all and then have to start over.

There will be two or three questions about each scenario. Follow the same process of reading the question and all four response options before answering a question and moving on to the next item.

Narrow Down the Choices

After you read the entire question and all the answers, you might feel confident that only one of the answers is right. If so, select it and move on. If you're not sure, use the strikeout feature in the testing platform to eliminate any responses you are certain don't answer the question, are incorrect, or don't make sense. That way, you can focus on the answers that are more likely to be right. If you are still unsure of the answer after rereading the item, you should make your best guess and then flag the item and return to it later.

Reread the Item as Needed

When in doubt, go back to the question and reread it. If you struggle with an item or think there is more than one correct answer, pause and reread the scenario (if it's an SJI) and question. Look for key words, HR terms, or other details that you might have missed when you first read it.

Keep in mind that it is normal to spend more time rereading toward the end of the exam. This might happen because (1) test fatigue starts to set in and you need to reread questions to make sure you understand them, or (2) you are reviewing items that you previously found challenging and flagged.

Once You've Decided on the Answer, Mentally Defend Your Choices

Know and understand why you chose your answer. Every knowledge item is developed by a SHRM-certified HR professional and must include a valid and verifiable reference and supporting rationale that explains why the correct answer is right. This ensures there is only one correct answer to every knowledge item on the exams. When you are answering an item, use the same process. Justify to yourself why you selected your answer as correct and why you eliminated each of the other options.

For situational judgment items, use specific information or details from the stem or scenario to support your thinking. In this case, you are looking for the *best* or *most effective* response presented. HR practitioners know that every situation in HR depends on variable factors, so there may not be a single universally *right way* to approach a given situation. In fact, you may not see the answer *you* would select present in the listing of four response options on the exam. It's critical to remember that you are looking for the *best* answer presented.

During this process, you'll sometimes realize you don't have a concrete reason for your choice. This does not mean your decision is wrong, but it is a sign that you might want to review the question again! Either reread the item to help you refine your thoughts or flag the item to return to it at the end of the section. Remember, HR handles things with shades of grey because everything depends on the situation. Therefore, the response options may not be 100 percent correct—but there is one that will stand out as the best or most effective option.

Use Your Time Wisely

The SHRM-CP and SHRM-SCP exams are timed, but they are not speed tests. You do not get extra points for finishing early. There is no need to rush. The test is designed to provide ample time to answer all the questions, and the vast majority of examinees finish their exam in the allotted time. However, if you spend too much time on one question, your time could run out before you're able to finish your exam. Don't watch the clock, but do periodically spot-check your time remaining.

This is where your experience and study come in. The more you know about the topics and the more practice questions you complete, the more confident you'll feel that you can answer all the questions within the allotted time.

If you finish the exam early, spend some extra time reviewing your answers. However, do not change an answer unless you are sure the first answer you selected is wrong.

There Is No Penalty for Guessing

No matter how well-prepared you are, some questions are bound to puzzle you. When this happens, don't panic or waste time reviewing the question over and over again. Remember that you receive credit for selecting the *correct* answer. If you guess, you have a 25 percent chance of getting it right—and an even better chance if you've eliminated the obviously wrong answers first. If you don't answer the question, you have a zero percent chance of getting it right—and it will count against your total score.

A good strategy is to strike out the obviously wrong responses, make an educated guess, and flag the question for later review.

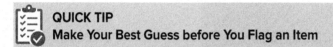

QUICK TIP
Make Your Best Guess before You Flag an Item

If you need to flag an item to return to later, make sure to choose an answer before you move on to the next question. In case you don't have time to return to it later, at least you haven't left it blank!

Once You Answer a Question, Move On

Don't waste time by second-guessing yourself. If you are not sure about an answer, mark the question for review and move on to the next. If you studied well and read both the question and the answer choices carefully, the odds are good that you will choose the right answer the first time. Resist the urge to change an answer unless you are confident you answered incorrectly when you first selected your answer.

Review Your Flagged Questions

Don't forget to revisit those challenging questions that you flagged. Once you answer all the questions, go back to those that you marked for review.

Just as before, be careful not to spend too much time on a single question or second-guess yourself. If you decide to change your answer to a question, use the process of mentally defending your choice to be certain you answered it wrong initially. Read more about checking flagged items in Chapter 11.

Stay Calm

Don't be afraid to take a moment to pause if you need it. Even if you feel confident that you are ready for the test, you still might feel panicky or rushed, and that can lead you to make mistakes. Take a moment to sit back, close your eyes, and take several deep breaths to calm yourself.

Strategies to Avoid

Not only did the item interviews reveal strategies that can help you perform well on a SHRM certification exam, but they also revealed strategies that should be avoided. In some situations, these strategies might slow you down a bit, while in others they could cause you to get answers wrong or even fail the exam.

We recommend avoiding these strategies while taking your exam. You should also avoid using them when you are taking practice questions or practice tests. Don't practice bad habits!

Avoid Trying to Predict the Answer Based on the Question

Trying to predict the answer—rather than focusing on the given response options—is not generally helpful because it wastes time. During the item interviews, many HR professionals said they wasted time trying to match one of the given response options to the answer they came up with in their head. This is particularly important to avoid for SJIs because there are many actions an HR professional could take and only four of them are listed as response options.

Predicting the answer based on the question can be a helpful strategy when facing a question at the recall level. For example, if you read the question and think, "X is the right method," you can look for that method among the answer choices. However, remember that only 15 to 20 percent of knowledge questions—or about 10 percent of all the questions—will be recall questions. Use this strategy judiciously, if at all.

Avoid Answering Based on Your Organization's Norms

The exam isn't designed to test information about *your* company, *your* industry, or *your* country. This means you should avoid selecting an answer simply
because it aligns with how a problem was resolved in your organization.
Instead, the SHRM certification exams are designed to assess how a competent HR professional who works anywhere in the world should act and what
information that professional should know. Use the best practices that are outlined in the SHRM BASK to guide your thinking.

Avoid Assuming a Response Option Is Correct Because It Is True

It is easy to assume that a statement you know to be true is the correct answer.
However, while an answer choice may be true in one context, it might not be
the right answer to the question that's being asked. Be sure to read the question and then select the response that best answers that specific question. In
other words, the response option needs to be both true and correctly answer
the question. For an SJI, this means making sure that the scenario supports the
answer you select. If a response option does not connect with the context of
the scenario, then you should eliminate it.

Avoid Analyzing What the Question *Meant* To Ask

You can waste a lot of time overthinking questions, especially SJIs. Keep in
mind all you have is the information given in the question. Do not insert information into the scenario or item if the information is not explicitly stated. Take
it at face value. While in real life, there might be different factors to consider
with different ways to approach a situation, your job is to answer the specific
question being asked. Do not overthink it or try to read into it; simply answer
the question that is presented.

Avoid Fixating on Details of the Scenario That Are Unrelated to a Question

You're not being tested on how many details in the scenarios you can remember, so don't waste time trying to memorize every detail of a scenario while
you read. In addition, there may be information in the scenario that helps you
better understand the situation and its context, or there may be information
that is missing because it is not necessary. Do not get hung up on what you
think is missing information, because it would be provided if it were necessary
to answer the question. Not every detail or phrase will be completely relevant
to the questions you are asked, and not every nuance of the situation will be

explained. Just like in real life, use the information you have available to you to make your best judgment. Don't allow contextual information to distract you from the question you are asked.

Avoid Looking for Clues Between Test Questions, Especially SJI Questions That Share a Scenario

The test questions on the SHRM certification exams are designed to stand alone, and one question will not give you a hint about another question. In fact, there is a specific step in the exam review process to make sure this does not occur.

Examinees are most likely to erroneously look for clues when answering SJIs. For SJIs, each scenario will have two or three associated questions that depend on that same scenario. However, each question is independent and does not rely on the other questions in the set. Because of this, do not try to use your answer to one question to answer another question or check to see how your answers flow together. For example, if you recommend revising a policy or strategic initiative in one question, don't assume that revision occurred when you answer other questions in the same set. You should answer each SJI question based only on the information in the scenario and that specific question

Avoid Changing Your Answer Because of a Pattern of Response Options

There's no pattern or sequence to correct answers. If you notice that you have selected a particular letter as the correct answer for several questions in a row (such as two, three, or even five Cs), resist the urge to change your answers. SHRM uses a general range of how often each of the four response options (A, B, C, D) can be used as the key, but there is no exact count. Trust your study and exam preparation, and always select the answer you feel is correct, regardless of whether it creates a pattern of response options.

Examples of Effectively Reasoning Through an Item

Phew, that's a lot! And all in three hours and forty minutes. So what does it look like to effectively and efficiently reason through an item? Let's look at two questions from the SHRM's item interview research as examples.

Reasoning through a KI Example

Let's start with a knowledge item and learn how successful test takers considered and answered the question. Remember, this is an exam item that is no longer used on SHRM-CP or SHRM-SCP exams, but it is representative of what examinees see on the exams today.

> 1. As a result of effectively promoting from within, organizations are most likely to spend comparatively more capital in which area?
>
>   A. Compensation
>
>   B. Talent acquisition
>
>   C. Learning and development
>
>   D. Onboarding

Successful test-takers typically read through the question first. Note that when we say "the question" here, we mean only the question and not the response options. Then they read the question a second time to check whether they missed anything. While reading, they identified key words, phrases, or HR terms that helped them better understand the question. The following words or phrases stood out to effective test takers:

» *Effectively promoting from within*: Successful test takers often defined this phrase in their own words as "promoting employees internally" or "moving employees around in an organization." Some test takers also defined the phrase by thinking about its opposite, which is bringing new hires into an organization.

» *More capital*: Successful test takers often defined this phrase in their own words as "spending more money" or "investing more money."

» *Most likely* and *comparatively*: Test takers keyed in on these key words to help them understand that the question was not about absolutes—it is about what organizations are likely to do.

By combining these key words and phrases together, successful test takers recognized that among the four options ("comparatively"), the correct response is the area in which organizations are most likely to spend more money ("capital") when promoting internally ("from within").

Next, successful test takers read through all four response options. After reading through the response options once, successful test takers began to assess and eliminate responses. While assessing each response option, successful test takers are able to state a rationale or explanation for why each response option was correct or incorrect. Here are the common rationales that we heard from successful test takers during the item interviews:

» A. *Compensation*: At first glance, this response option is about money ("capital"), so it could be correct. However, it is traditionally more expensive to hire externally than it is to promote internally. A promoted employee who is brand new to a role will likely fall toward the lower end of a pay scale, while a new hire may have more experience and therefore earn higher compensation.

» B. *Talent acquisition*: Internal promotions do not require new talent acquisition efforts because the talent already exists in the organization. There are often lower costs associated with posting an open position for internal promotion, and the process of identifying talent requires fewer resources than recruiting a new employee externally. In fact, an organization is more likely to spend less capital on talent acquisition when promoting from within, so this response option doesn't make sense.

» C. *Learning and development*: Money that is spent on learning and development helps current employees grow and enhance the skills necessary to perform their role well and prepare for their next role. It makes sense to invest money into an employee to help them grow, and a newly promoted employee may require extra developmental support as the employee gains the knowledge, skills, and abilities to succeed at the higher level position. This answer makes sense.

» D. *Onboarding*: Onboarding occurs at the beginning of the employee life cycle. Because this question asks about internal promotions, the employee likely already went through the onboarding process. Based on this reasoning, this answer does not make sense because there would be no onboarding necessary when conducting an internal promotion.

By following this thinking, successful test takers correctly reasoned that C is the correct answer. The most important key words or phrases were "more capital" and "promoting from within," and C aligned with this well

Reasoning Through an SJI Example

The process for reasoning through an SJI is similar, although a bit more time-consuming because there is more to read and understand. Let's see how successful test takers approach answering this type of question. Remember, this is a real exam item that is no longer used on either the SHRM-CP or SHRM-SCP exam, but it is representative of items on current exams.

Successful test takers read through the scenario first:

An engagement survey at a global company reveals a widespread issue with the perceived fairness of the internal hiring process. According to the survey results, many employees feel the process is biased because candidates from the department with an open vacancy are typically selected over candidates from different departments, despite similar qualifications and competencies. This is because most departments in the company prefer to promote from within to keep employees engaged and ensure minimal investment in development for their roles.

To support inclusion and diversity, the CEO requires all employees have the opportunity to apply for posted positions. For each posted position, hundreds of internal candidates apply. Many internal candidates do not meet the technical requirements of a role. Hiring managers are required to interview at least 10 candidates, and they complain this takes a significant amount of time away from their other duties.

After reading the scenario, successful test takers paused to think about and summarize what they read. They also considered their initial gut reactions to what they read. For example, during the item interviews many successful test takers remarked that interviewing at least ten candidates seemed excessive and time-consuming.

After they were sure they understood the information that was described in the scenario, they moved on to the question. Remember that when we say "the question," we mean only the question and not the response options.

2. Which action should HR take to immediately reduce bias in the process while maintaining the corporate culture of inclusiveness?

    A. Lower the minimum technical requirements for job vacancies.

    B. Create interview and inclusiveness training for hiring managers.

    C. Draft a plan to implement cross-departmental panel interviews.

    D. Limit the number of internal hires from within a department.

While reading, successful test takers identified key words, phrases, or HR terms that helped them better understand the question. The following words or phrases stood out to successful test takers:

» *Reduce bias*: Using the information in both the scenario and the stem, successful test takers generally defined this phrase in their own words as "minimizing the preference that interviewers had toward employees from the same department."

» *Maintain a culture of inclusiveness*: Using the information in both the scenario and the stem, successful test takers generally defined this phrase in their own words as "giving employees equal opportunity to apply for new roles, regardless of department."

» *While*: Test takers keyed in on this word to help them understand that the question is about balance. The HR professional in the scenario needs to simultaneously reduce bias and maintain a culture of inclusiveness.

» *Immediately*: Successful test takers clued in on this word as a term related to hierarchy and often defined this phrase in their own words as the action that an HR professional should take to "have an effect right away" or "have an effect most quickly." Many correctly predicted that several of the response options might be effective at reducing bias and maintaining inclusiveness but that the correct one would have the most immediate effect.

Next, successful test takers read through all four response options. After reading through the response options once, successful test takers began to eliminate response options while rereading them to further assess each option.

While assessing each response option, successful test takers could think of a rationale or explanation for why each response option was correct or incorrect. Here are the common rationales that we heard from successful test takers during the item interviews:

» A. *Lower the minimum technical requirements for job vacancies.* The scenario and question are focused on bias in the process and not technical qualifications. Reducing technical qualifications is not a good idea because employees will not be able to perform required job duties. This is not an effective action.

» B. *Create interview and inclusiveness training for hiring managers.* This is an effective action that can help improve the interview process and increase inclusiveness. However, this action would not produce immediate results because it would take time to get stakeholder approval, create the training, and deliver it to hiring managers. Due to the timing, this is not the best answer.

» C. *Draft a plan to implement cross-departmental panel interviews.* Using cross-departmental panel interviews is an effective action to reduce bias and increase inclusiveness. Also, it would take less investment than creating interview and inclusiveness training. However, this action would not produce immediate results because it would take time to get draft a plan that describes the new process, get stakeholder approval, and implement the process. Due to the timing, this is not the best answer.

» D. *Limit the number of internal hires from within a department.* Because this action is similar to a quota, this can be implemented quickly and therefore produces the most immediate results. It reduces bias by not allowing hiring managers to only hire from within a department, which gives employees a more equal opportunity to apply and be selected.

Successful test takers correctly reasoned that D is the correct answer. This item is a great example of the importance of reading carefully. During the item interviews, many seasoned HR professionals picked B or C because these are generally effective workplace strategies. However, these do not address the need for an immediate solution and are therefore not the best answer.

Chapter 10

Manage Test Anxiety and Push Through Procrastination

I've had a lot of worries in my life, most of which never happened.

—Mark Twain

Have you ever felt nervous or anxious before or during an important test? How did those feelings manifest themselves? Some describe anxiety as causing troubles with sleep cycles, shaking hands, upset stomach, accelerated heartbeat, difficulty breathing, lack of concentration, and panicking.

If you've ever felt nervous or anxious before or during a test, you are not alone. Taking a test is a form of performance, and performers of all kinds, from professional actors and musicians to conference presenters, often feel the symptoms of performance anxiety, or stage fright.

Even though you don't have to stand up in front of people to take a professional test like the SHRM-CP or SHRM-SCP exam, you are being asked to demonstrate what you know. It is common for test takers to worry that they will not be able to perform well. The stakes are high; therefore, the anxiety is greater. For many people, a little anxiety can be a good thing. It can increase your focus and concentration and help you to do your best. However, for others, anxiety can lead to feelings of panic that result in what they most fear: failure.

The good news is that most test takers experience only mild symptoms that they can manage easily by understanding what causes their anxiety and learning how to reduce it. Even if you have a history of performance anxiety, you'll find that the strategies in this section can help you manage your symptoms, so you can focus your attention where it belongs: on the exam.

Understanding Test Anxiety

Test anxiety manifests itself in a variety of ways. The symptoms can vary considerably and range from mild to severe. Most of us have felt at least some of these symptoms at one time or another. You can't concentrate, and your mind races with negative thoughts. You have trouble sleeping. You feel nauseous; your mouth is dry, and your hands are sweaty and shaking; your heart races.

Those symptoms have a physical basis: they come from what psychologists call the *fight or flight response*. When faced with a real or imaginary threat, the body releases adrenaline to prepare itself to either fight or run away from the threat. That was very useful when we were threatened by predators in the wild. It is not so helpful when preparing to take a certification exam.

Test anxiety can also create a type of noise in your brain that makes it difficult to recall information from your memory. That noise can make it hard to understand test questions and make reasoned judgments about which responses to select.

Acknowledging that test anxiety can occur is the first step in preparing yourself to manage it effectively.

Strategies for Reducing Test Anxiety
Build Your Confidence by Preparing Thoroughly

Cutting corners just doesn't cut it. A certification exam is a serious undertaking and preparing for it is crucial. The better you know and understand the material, the more you will feel confident in your ability to pass. That confidence makes it far less likely that high levels of test anxiety could get in the way of your success.

Being familiar with how the exam is structured and how the exam platform works can also increase your confidence. Reading about each type of question on the exam; completing the exam's in-platform tutorial to see how its features (such as highlighting and strikethrough) work and how the platform displays items on the screen; and prereading the candidate agreement can help you be more confident about what to expect during the exam. You can also talk to other HR professionals who took the SHRM certification exam to learn about their experiences and their approaches to exam preparation.

Don't wait until the last minute. Try not to overprepare, but make sure you are comfortable with the subjects that might be tested on the exam, and allow yourself time to reflect on your work experiences. To learn what concepts may appear on the exam read through the SHRM Body of Applied Skills and Knowledge (SHRM BASK) on the SHRM Certification's Exam Preparation webpage: https://www.shrm.org/credentials/certification/exam-preparation/body-of-applied-skills-and-knowledge.

There is no replacement for preparation. Embrace this simple truth and act accordingly.

Reinforce Positive Thinking

The anxious mind is very busy, and not in a good way. Test anxiety brings with it lots of negative thoughts that make it hard to think clearly. Thinking that you cannot possibly pass the exam does not mean you are destined to fail.

When those negative thoughts enter your mind, take a step back to examine them and rebuke false narratives. Why do you think the test is too difficult for you? Why do you think that you won't be able to pass? Why are you predicting that you will not do well? After examining negative thoughts more objectively, remind yourself that you have worked hard to prepare yourself for success.

Every time a negative thought comes up, look at it rationally and tell yourself, "Yes, it's a challenging exam, but I am prepared to do my very best!" The power of positive thinking can help reshape your confidence and reduce the negative thoughts that anxiety brings. Saying, writing down, or thinking positive affirmations like, "I am capable of handling anything" or simply, "All problems have solutions" before beginning a study session can link positivity with your preparation! Reinforcing your capabilities will help boost your confidence, which will help in warding off any manifestations of anxiety.

> Consider this: thinking something will or will not happen does not make it real.

Keep a Journal

One popular approach to help manage anxiety is to write down your thoughts and feelings as test day approaches. Writing about stressful events can improve the ability to learn, solve problems, and more. Some have found this type of expressive writing influences the capacity of their working memory.

Whether you choose to journal on paper or electronically, find a quiet place to record your thoughts and feelings in the weeks before test day. When you find yourself thinking negative thoughts, write them down, think about what is causing your negative thoughts, reason through them, and visualize success instead. Use the journal as a place to release any negative thoughts and imagine those thoughts now trapped on the pages. With the negative thoughts contained in the journal, you can move forward to reinforce positive thinking.

Learn How to Calm Yourself

Even if you prepare thoroughly and feel confident that you know the material, you may suddenly feel nervous or anxious before or during the exam. Learning how to calm yourself can help you concentrate. Try these techniques well before test day. Practice them early and access them when you need them.

» *Breathe slowly and deeply.* Experience shows that rapid and shallow breathing can make you feel tense. Learn to calm your breathing. Take several slow, deep breaths and let them out evenly and slowly. Count each inhale and exhale to focus your mind on a single action before continuing.

» *Tense, then relax your muscles.* Tightness in the shoulders and other muscle groups is a common response to stress. Practice relaxing your body. Shrug or roll your shoulders, open your mouth to unclench your jaw, and gently roll your head from side to side or around in circles. If you do these kinds of exercises a few times daily, you will remember to use them if you start to feel tense in the exam room.

» *Visualize.* Find a quiet place and close your eyes. Visualize yourself entering the test space, sitting down in front of the computer, and completing the test. Further visualize success by picturing yourself holding your SHRM-certified certificate in your hands.

» *Participate in activities that help you manage stress.* Studying for the exam is an intense process, and it can be helpful to do activities that help you feel calmer or lower stress. You know yourself best; engage in healthy activities that help you relax most, such as spending time in nature or with a friend.

Be Ready for Test Day

Don't deviate too far from your normal routine before test day. Be sure to get a good night's rest and eat a filling meal before your scheduled exam time. You are unlikely to feel relaxed if you spend all night before the test studying, if you have to rush to get to the testing center on time, or you did not check your computer's capabilities before attempting to launch the exam at home.

If you are taking the exam in person, make sure you know how to get to the test center, and plan to get there early so you do not feel rushed. When you arrive, engage with the proctor.

If you are taking the exam via remote proctor, make sure you know how to log into the testing platform, confirm your internet connection is secure, and give yourself extra time to virtually connect with the proctor so you do not feel rushed. Prepare for the security check ahead of time to ensure your space is approved for remote testing. Review all provided information regarding setting up your remote testing space and do so well before your scheduled exam appointment. Confirm that your space will be free of interruptions, such as animals, cohabitors, or family members, before launching your exam. When you launch the platform, be patient while waiting to connect with the proctor. The time spent during the initial security screening before starting the exam does not take away from the amount of time you have to complete the exam. If you do choose to take your optional break, you will be required to complete a new security check and the clock will not stop running.

Envision Success

Picture this: after you take the exam, you receive a preliminary letter that states, "Congratulations. You passed." Manifest this success by establishing a roadmap. Plan well and allow enough time to prepare for your exam experience. When you get to the test center or launch the exam remotely, take a deep breath and leverage exam-preparation focus strategies to dispel anxieties.

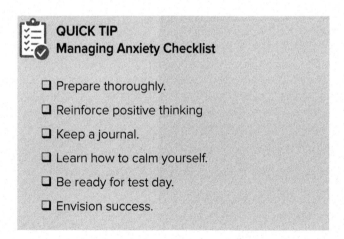

QUICK TIP
Managing Anxiety Checklist

☐ Prepare thoroughly.

☐ Reinforce positive thinking

☐ Keep a journal.

☐ Learn how to calm yourself.

☐ Be ready for test day.

☐ Envision success.

Requesting An Accommodation

SHRM celebrates and recognizes individuals' uniqueness that they bring to our community. Attaining SHRM certification is a significant achievement, and SHRM understands that individual circumstances could lead to questions about taking the SHRM exam(s). Candidates may request a testing accommodation (see Chapter 11), which will be reviewed by SHRM. All testing accommodation requests are treated as confidential information.

For further information on requesting a testing accommodation for the SHRM-CP and SHRM-SCP exams, please refer to the SHRM Certification Handbook: https://www.shrm.org/credentials/certification/shrm-certification-handbook.

Pushing Through Procrastination

Do any of these statements describe the way you usually approach challenging projects?

❑ I spend a lot of time thinking about how to get started.

❑ I keep thinking that I'll get to it, and suddenly the deadline is staring me in the face.

❑ I work better at the last minute, so I put it off as long as possible.

These are common indicators of procrastination. Many people procrastinate periodically. For some people, however, procrastination is a lifelong problem. This behavior can take on various forms, but the general theme is leaving things until the very last minute, postponing studying, and struggling to meet deadlines. There is a cost associated with procrastination: decreased performance and increased anxiety. Objectively, procrastinating makes no sense: your rational mind knows it is self-defeating. However, recognizing common reasons for procrastination and learning to manage that tendency can help you change your behavior to accomplish your goals.

We Procrastinate When We Are Overwhelmed

Imagine you have been asked to move your entire department of twenty-five people to a new building. Big, important projects like this can be overwhelming. "There is so much to do," you might think. "It's too much for me to tackle." Studying for an important exam like the SHRM-CP or the SHRM-SCP can feel the same way.

What to Do

To tackle any big project, break it down into a series of manageable tasks—it's much easier to do a series of tasks than to try doing everything at once. In fact, this is the purpose of a study plan.

Your study plan is like the detailed plan a contractor follows to build the home shown in the architect's blueprints. It includes specific goals, action steps for achieving them, and a timetable for taking each action. Breaking down the process into manageable units makes the whole task less daunting. If you get off track, take a breath and readjust. Don't use one missed study session as an excuse to throw out the entire study plan.

We Procrastinate When We Have Trouble Managing Our Time

Everyone is very busy these days. There never seems to be enough time. Things always take longer than expected, and to-do lists keep growing. It can even be a major challenge to think about finding the time to study.

What to Do

One thing is certain: you cannot add more time to a day. What you can do is spend that time wisely. Try keeping a time log. A time log helps to show how you spend your time so you can manage it more effectively.

Whether you use a notepad, a spreadsheet, or an app on your phone to set up your time log, as soon as you track all your activities for a week, you will see a pattern emerge of how you spend your time. Include time at work, commuting time, time with family, non-work time, socializing . . . *everything*.

Your time log will help you become aware of how you really use your time. You might notice that something you thought took a couple of hours actually took less than an hour to complete. Consider whether you spend time doing things that do not need to be done or that could be done more efficiently. Thinking about these things will help you set priorities and reserve the time you need for study

We Might Procrastinate Because We Fear Failure —or Success

A common reason for procrastinating is the fear of failing. Why try if you can't succeed? This thinking can apply to studying for an exam. Why study if you think you have no chance of passing? Surprisingly, success can also bring new challenges, higher performance expectations, more pressure, and more stress. That can be scary. It can feel easier not to put in the effort in the first place.

A related reason for procrastination is the fear of not doing something perfectly. Achieving perfection is like trying to scale a wall that gets higher and higher as you climb. If you feel that there's no way to get over the top, why bother?

What to Do

Become aware of your fears and how they obstruct the path toward your goals. Remember that both failures and successes are opportunities to learn and grow.

Instead of worrying about the bad things that could happen if you fail the SHRM certification exam, think about the good things that will come when you are certified. Focus on why certification is important to you. Think about the ways in which being certified will benefit you in your career as an HR professional. The more certain you are about the value of passing the test, the easier it will be to make studying for it a priority.

We Procrastinate Because It Has Become a Habit

Experienced procrastinators have honed the fine art of distracting themselves, sometimes even justifying it. Instead of working, they check their phones and email, think about what to have for dinner, find someone to chat with, rearrange their workspace, browse the internet, clean out the refrigerator, and do myriad other time-wasting things. Then they look up at the clock and wonder where all the time has gone.

For some, procrastination has become a bad habit and stopping any bad habit takes a determined effort. It doesn't happen overnight.

What to Do

Write down all the ways in which you distract yourself while you are working or studying. Post the list prominently in your workspace or study space and add to it if you find a new distraction.

When you begin a study session, remove the obvious distractors such as your phone and internet access. Make yourself comfortable with water, coffee, or a snack close at hand if needed. Whenever you think about or do something other than studying, stop for a moment, take a deep breath, remind yourself of how important it is to achieve your goals, and then turn your attention back to your study plan.

While studying, set reasonable time goals to dedicate to it. If you have a habit of procrastinating, setting a study goal of studying three hours at a time every day without distraction may contribute to feeling overwhelmed and induce more procrastination.

Focus on positive reinforcement. Breaking a bad habit can also be easier when you reward yourself for your accomplishments. Give yourself a reward when you reach milestones on your study plan. Put some money each week into a rewards jar to spend after you reach your final goal: taking the certification exam.

> **QUICK TIP**
> **Strategies to Overcome Procrastination**
>
> ❑ Determine why you procrastinate.
> ❑ Break projects into manageable tasks or chunks.
> ❑ Learn to manage your time.
> ❑ Remove distractors.
> ❑ Focus on what you want to achieve.
> ❑ Reward yourself for your achievements.

Part 4

Exam Day

*The only limit to our realization of tomorrow
will be our doubts of today.*

—Franklin D. Roosevelt

Chapter 11

What to Expect on Exam Day

Nothing is impossible, the word itself says 'I'm possible'!

—Audrey Hepburn

You've worked diligently to prepare for the certification exam, and now the big day is almost here. Knowing what to expect can help you feel more comfortable and less nervous. Your experience on exam day depends somewhat on how you choose to take your exam. If you choose to take the exam in person, your SHRM certification exam will be held at one of Prometric's highly secure testing centers. If you choose to take the exam via remote proctoring, you will take the exam from the comfort of your own home or office using Prometric's ProProctor system.

Whichever testing method and certification exam you choose, the format of your exam and the level of test security will be the same on test day.

In-Person Testing

Prometric operates hundreds of test centers in more than fifty countries, typically in secure testing centers located in office buildings and on college campuses. If you choose to take your exam in-person at a Prometric test center, follow these tips to help ensure a smooth experience.

Get to the Test Center Early

It's essential to arrive at the test center on time. The test center administrator (TCA) can deny access to individuals who arrive late for an exam. If that happens, you'll need to reapply for the exam and pay another fee. You do not want to do this!

Arrive at the test center at least thirty minutes early so you can park, locate the test center area, take a bio break, check in, and be ready to go when your exam starts. It's a good idea to do a dry run a few days before your exam: drive or take public transportation to the test center and note how long it takes you. If you drive there, figure out where to park. Leave extra time in case traffic is heavy or public transit is slow on test day.

Checking in at the Test Center

When you arrive at the test center, the TCA will check you in. The TCA will ask you to show a valid photo identification (ID) and sign a logbook. Be sure you reread your Authorization-to-Test (ATT) letter and review the Prometric website about acceptable forms of ID. Your photo ID must be current, so check it far in advance of your test date in case it is about to expire.

You can expect a high level of security inside the testing center (not unlike the security you encounter at an airport). Bring only what you need into the testing center because you'll need to leave all your personal belongings except your ID, eyeglasses, and locker key in a locker. This includes your phone and any jewelry except wedding and engagement rings.

Before you enter the testing room, the TCA will inspect your eyeglasses, hair clips, ties, face coverings, and any other accessories to look for camera devices that could be used to capture exam content. It's a good idea to leave such items as ornate clips, combs, barrettes, headbands, tie clips, and cuff links behind because you might not be allowed to wear them into the testing room. The TCA might ask you to turn out your pockets, and you might also be wanded or asked to go through a metal detector.

Although these inspections are thorough, they take only a few minutes. They will be repeated when you return from a break to ensure you do not violate any security protocols.

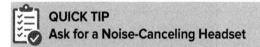

QUICK TIP
Ask for a Noise-Canceling Headset

Blocking out noise can help you concentrate during the exam. If you would like to minimize the sounds around you during your exam, you can ask for a noise-canceling headset when you check in.

Your Exam Computer and Station

Once you are checked in, the TCA will guide you to a seat at an exam computer. Make yourself comfortable and familiarize yourself with the feel of the keyboard and mouse. Use the time before the exam starts to take the exam tutorial so you'll be familiar with the test platform navigation functions, especially the features for striking out obviously incorrect responses and marking or flagging questions you want to return to for review.

FYI
Not Only SHRM Test Takers Are Testing

Not everyone at the testing center will be taking a SHRM certification exam. In fact, the person on one side of you might be taking an accounting exam while the person on your other side might be taking a cosmetology exam. The various exams are likely to take differing amounts of time, so you can expect that people taking other exams will come and go during your exam period.

Live Remote Proctoring

If you select to take your exam via live remote proctoring, you will receive an appointment confirmation email with important information and links. Take time at least one day before your scheduled exam date to read through the information, (re)complete the system compatibility check, and download the ProProctor application.

You should expect a high level of security during your exam, just as if you were taking the exam in-person at a Prometric test center.

Prepare Your Testing Room In Advance

During a remote-proctored exam, the room where you take your exam *becomes* a test center. Because of this, your testing environment is subject to strict rules to ensure the security of the exam content.

When you are selecting and preparing your testing environment, keep in mind:

» Your testing locations must be indoors (walled), be well lit, have a closed door, and be free from background noise and disruptions.

» The entrance to the room must be in full view of the camera.

» Your workstation and surrounding area, including the walls, must be free of materials such as pictures, office supplies, or electronic devices.

Start preparing your testing environment at least a few hours ahead of time by tidying up and removing prohibited items from the room. This includes cleaning off your desk and removing extra technology, like a docking station or extra monitors. If you are unable to remove a larger item from the room, such as a bookcase full of books, use a sheet or other linen to cover it.

(Re)take the System Readiness Check

You should have taken the system readiness check before deciding to use remote proctoring. Take a few minutes before your exam date to rerun it (or if you didn't run it before, to run it for the first time). This readiness check lets you know whether your operating system is compatible to install and run ProProctor, which is the application that delivers remote proctored exams from Prometric

Once your compatibility check is complete, enter your confirmation number and surname to download the ProProctor application. If you downloaded the application previously, enter your confirmation details to ensure you have the most up-to-date software.

Log In to Your Exam

Just before you log in, do a final check of your testing environment. Remove all unnecessary items or personal belongings from the room, such as books and extra technology. This includes your cell phone! You are not allowed to have your cell phone in the room during your exam. Consider placing your cell phone just outside of the closed door so that you can quickly access it if you run into technology issues during your exam.

Make sure to remove any jewelry you are wearing as well, except wedding and engagement rings. Keep only what you need in the room where you plan to take your exam, including your computer, ID, and eyeglasses.

Once you log into the ProProctor system, you will first complete an identification check. This will include taking a digital picture of your valid photo ID. Be sure you reread your ATT letter and review the information on the Prometric website about acceptable forms of ID. Your photo ID must be current, so check it far in advance of your test date in case it is about to expire.

Although these inspections are thorough, they take only a few minutes. If you take a break during the exam, an inspection will be repeated when you return from your break to ensure you are still in compliance with the security protocols.

Once your security check is complete, you will be passed on to your proctor. Your testing session will be monitored by a qualified proctor through audio-video and screen-share feed in real time. If you need assistance during your exam or wish to take an unscheduled break, type a chat to your proctor.

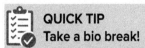

QUICK TIP
Take a bio break!

It's a good idea to use the bathroom before you begin your exam. The certification exam is four hours long, and there are no scheduled breaks. You may take one unscheduled break if you need it, but you will have to go through security again and will not be given extra time on the exam. That said, if you have extra time at the end of the first half of your exam, it might be a good idea to take an unscheduled break to use the restroom, splash water on your face, stretch, or loosen up tense shoulders.

Acceptable Forms of Identification

Be sure you read your ATT letter and review the Prometric website to learn about acceptable forms of ID. Your photo ID must be current, so check it far in advance of your test date in case it is about to expire (Table 11.1).

Table 11.1. Acceptable Forms of Identification

Primary ID	Secondary ID
Driver's license	Valid employer identification card
Passport	Valid credit card with signature
Military ID	Valid bank card with photo

Examples of Acceptable and Unacceptable Names on Application

Name on Application	Name on ID	Admitted to Test?
Jamie Taylor-Smith	Jamie Smith	Yes
Nancy Porter	Nancy White	No
William B. Johnson	Bill Johnson	No
P. J. Miller	Peter J. Miller	Yes
Samantha R. Roberts	Samantha Rose Roberts	Yes

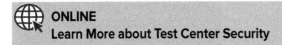

ONLINE
Learn More about Test Center Security

https://www.prometric.com/test-center-security

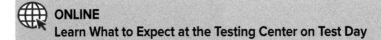

ONLINE
Learn What to Expect at the Testing Center on Test Day

https://www.prometric.com/prepare-for-test-day

https://www.prometric.com/test-takers/what-expect

Testing Accommodations

SHRM is fully committed to ensuring access to the SHRM-CP and SHRM-SCP certification exams for all individuals with disabilities covered by the Americans with Disabilities Act (or the Canadian or Australian equivalent).

SHRM provides reasonable accommodations to individuals with documented disabilities who demonstrate a need for special accommodations. Requests for special accommodations are inherently individualized and considered on a case-by-case basis. Therefore, no single type of accommodation will be appropriate for all individuals with disabilities. Common accommodation requests include extended time (either time-and-a-half or double-time) or testing in a separate room to reduce distractions.

All accommodation requests must be made at the time of application for an exam. To request an accommodation, the individual seeking an accommodation must complete a form and have a qualified licensed professional complete the evaluation. The professional must be an individual qualified to assess, diagnose, and treat the stated disability. Any information and documentation provided regarding the disability and the need for accommodation in testing will be kept strictly confidential and will be shared only to the extent necessary with our testing vendor.

For more information about testing accommodations, see the SHRM Certification Handbook at https://www.shrm.org/credentials/certification/shrm-certification-handbook.

Rescheduling Your Exam

If you can't make your original test date, you can reschedule the exam for a fee payable to Prometric. If you cancel less than five days before the test or fail to show up at your scheduled time, you will forfeit the fees and will need to reapply for another exam window (Table 11.2).

Table 11.2. Rescheduling Exam Appointments

Time Frame	Reschedule Permitted	Stipulations
Requests submitted **thirty days** or more before original appointment	Yes	Candidate must pay Prometric a cancellation fee of $35.00.
Requests submitted **five to twenty-nine days** before original appointment	Yes	Candidate must pay Prometric a cancellation fee of $53.00.
Requests submitted **less than five days** before original appointment	No	Candidate is considered a no-show, will forfeits all fees, and will have to reapply and pay the fees for a future exam window.

In cases of extreme weather or a national emergency, Prometric may need to cancel the exam. In that case, Prometric will reschedule you as soon as possible, and you won't be charged a fee for rescheduling.

Top Tips for Test Day

Before Your Exam

» **Get a good night's sleep the night before your exam.** Do not cram the night before your exam.

» **Eat a light, healthy meal.** Aim for a well-rounded meal that includes protein, carbohydrates, and fats to keep your energy steady during the exam.

» **Use the restroom.**

» **Plan out your break.** Remember, the clock keeps ticking even while you are on your break!

> ˃ If you are taking your exam at a Prometric test center, ask where the restroom is located when you arrive. If you take a break to use the restroom during your exam, knowing how to access the restroom minimizes the amount of time you are away from your test.

> ˃ If you are taking your exam via remote proctor, place water and food outside your exam room so you can grab it quickly.

During Your Exam

» **Use your test-taking tips and relaxation strategies.** Take deep calming breaths as needed. Stay focused and think positively. Keep the other strategies mentioned in Part 3 in mind as you complete your exam.

» **Keep your eye on the time.** Once you begin your exam, there will be a timer on every screen to remind you about how much time you have left for that section. Do not rush through the exam, but look at the timer periodically to make sure you are still on track.

» **Use the relevant features in the exam interface.** Use the virtual scratch-pad feature to make notes or write down key information as needed. Use the highlight and strikethrough features as you read the test questions to help you select the right answer. Use the on-screen calculator for any calculations.

» **Be thoughtful about when you choose to take your break.** Let's say that you just finished the first half of your exam and checked all your flagged items. You kept up a good pace as you answered questions, and you have about twenty minutes of your one hour and fifty minutes left for the first section. On to the second half, right? Not so fast! **Consider taking a break.**

» The exam time clock continues to run while you are on a break regardless of where you are in the exam, and **any remaining time in section 1 does not roll over to the next section**. In this scenario, you could take a fifteen-minute break and still have five minutes of exam time left (minus time spent going through the security check) before moving into the second half.

» **Spend your break time wisely.** Splash water on your face if it feels good or helps refresh you. Spend a few minutes moving your body if you want, such as taking a short walk outdoors. If you are taking the exam remotely, this could also mean doing a few yoga stretches or even playing with a pet. Give your brain a few minutes to decompress.

After Your Exam

No matter the results, reward yourself for finishing the exam! Taking a SHRM certification exam is hard work. Regardless of your result, take time to celebrate your effort with a delicious meal, time off from work, a new (non-HR related!) book, or another meaningful activity or reward. You deserve it!

Chapter 12

During and After Your Exam

*Success is not final; failure is not fatal: It is
the courage to continue that counts.*

—Winston S. Churchill

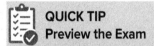

QUICK TIP
Preview the Exam

You can preview the exam tutorial ahead of time from your home or office computer. The tutorial explains the various features and lets you practice answering questions as well as using the features for striking out responses and flagging questions for review. You can access the tutorial at the website below:

https://www.prometric.com/sites/default/files/SHRM-Tutorial/launch_assessment_delivery.html

During Your Exam

As you take the exam, use the strategies and tips in Chapter 10 to manage your time and stay relaxed. If you need help or need to take a break, let Prometric know. If you are in a Prometric testing center, raise your hand and the TCA will come over. If you are taking the exam via remote proctor, send a message to your proctor using the chat feature.

Timing the Exam

The total exam time is four hours, including opening and closing activities. You will have three hours and forty minutes to answer the 134 multiple-choice questions on the exam itself. The exam is divided into two halves, so you will have one hour and fifty minutes to answer the first 67 multiple-choice questions and another one hour and fifty minutes to answer the second 67 multiple-choice questions. Make sure you review all flagged or unanswered items before you finish each half. Once you finish the first half, you won't be able to go back to it later.

The countdown timer on the screen will help you keep track of the time as you progress through the two sections. You cannot carry over unused time from one section and save it to use in another section. For example, if you have fifteen minutes left at the end of the first half, you will still only have one hour and fifty minutes to answer the questions in the second half. You cannot carry those unused fifteen minutes over to the second half.

Although it's important to stay aware of the time, you don't need to feel rushed. SHRM research shows that the vast majority of examinees have enough time to complete the exam without rushing, and almost everyone completes all of the items. You will have enough time to answer all the questions and take another look at those you've marked for review.

Pay Attention to Pop-up Messages on the Screen and Don't Click on "Finish" until You're Done!

Pop-up warnings often occur when you've hit a stray key and the computer thinks you want to finish the exam. The system asks you at least twice to confirm that you understand that if you keep clicking "Yes," you want to finish. Also, the "Finish" button in the navigation bar does not finish your review of the questions you've flagged for another look—it ends the entire exam. After you click "Finish," a pop-up window will appear asking you to confirm that you are done.

DO NOT end the exam until you are sure that you are finished. You cannot return to it once you exit. When a pop-up appears, pause, read it thoroughly, and then click the button that indicates what you want to do. DO NOT rush through the prompts, because each asks you to confirm your real intent but in a slightly different way.

If, after multiple warnings, you exit the exam, but did not mean to do so, there is no turning back. Once you confirm, you are at the point of no return and the exam will be over.

When You Finish Your Exam

Once your exam time is up or you hit "Finish" and confirmed that you are done, a short post-exam survey will appear on your screen. The brief survey helps SHRM learn more about test takers' opinions about the exam, reasons for pursuing certification, study and preparation methods, and current jobs. Your responses to survey questions do _not_ affect your test results.

After you finish the survey, the system will give you an immediate "Pass" or "Did Not Pass" notification. This notification is preliminary and subject to a post exam score verification review. Prometric will also send you a copy of the results by email. Be sure to check your spam folder if the email doesn't arrive.

Regardless of the results, congratulate yourself! Completing this rigorous test is a significant accomplishment, and you deserve a reward for all your hard work, so do something nice for yourself!

After Your Exam: Next Steps

Your Official Score Report

About two to three weeks after your exam, you will receive an email from SHRM about your official SHRM-CP or SHRM-SCP score report. An electronic copy of your official score report will be posted in your SHRM portal account. This report includes your scaled score (from 120 to 200), as well as feedback on how well you scored on the three knowledge domains (people, organization, and workplace) and three competency clusters (interpersonal, leadership, and business). You can use this information to plan professional activities that support your learning and earn credits toward your recertification.

If you did not pass the exam, you can use this information to refocus your study plan to retake the SHRM-CP or SHRM-SCP exam in a future testing window.

You Passed! Your SHRM-Certified Certificate and Digital Badge

A soft copy of your new SHRM certification certificate will also be posted in your SHRM portal account with your official results report. You will also receive an email from Credly issuing your digital badge. You must accept the digital badge in order to share it on social media, such as on LinkedIn.

You Passed! Maintain Your Certification through Recertification

Achieving certification sets you on the path to continuous learning and career development. Maintaining your certification helps you keep your knowledge, skills, and abilities relevant.

To maintain your certification, you can either retest or earn sixty professional development credits (PDCs) within each three-year period. Recertifying by earning PDCs is the most popular option. Credits are awarded for your study, your experience, and your contributions in three categories: education, profession, and your organization. There are more than 110,000 opportunities with over 3,100 providers to earn PDCs, including attending events, volunteering, completing major work projects, and reading books. You can also earn recertification by retaking the certification exam.

Although you can earn all sixty credits by attending virtual or in-person professional development programs, many certified professionals also choose to document a major work project completed and endorsed by their supervisor to earn up to thirty PDCs. You can also earn up to thirty PDCs in the *advance your profession* category. This includes things like completing a survey, making a presentation, or publishing an article or book chapter.

When you are planning your recertification strategy, don't overlook the importance of volunteering. Serving in a volunteer leadership role or even as a volunteer supporting SHRM item-writing activities for future exams is an important way to supplement your professional development education and earn PDCs.

Visit the SHRM recertification page online to learn more about recertification and other types of activities that qualify for PDCs.

 ONLINE

Learn about the various categories, what kind of documentation to submit, and how many PDCs can be earned by category: https://www.shrm.org/credentials/certification/recertification/qualifying-activities.

On behalf of the entire SHRM team around the globe, we wish you good luck on the SHRM certification exam. Visualize success and you can succeed!

Appendixes

Appendix 1

Twenty-Five Top Test-Taking Tips

SHRM collected the top test-taking tips from SHRM-certified HR profession-als as well as subject matter experts who support the development of the exams. Use these ideas to refine your study plan and set yourself up for success on exam day!

1. Make this test one of your main priorities for several months before the test! If you have other major life events occurring around the same time, it might not be the best time to try and fit this in.

2. Set aside time to study, and prepare your family for the time commitment proper preparation will require.

3. Study the SHRM BASK!

4. Take an in-person or virtual SHRM Learning System prep course.

5. Understand that there is *no way* to retain all the information covered in the materials. Memorize principles, not facts.

6. Connect with a local learning group for the SHRM test preparation.

7. Know your study style, plan your study strategy, and stick to the plan.

8. Use SHRM-developed practice tests and practice questions to help you prepare.

9. Understand the scenarios in order to apply the best approach.

10. Understand the concept to apply it (not just the definition).

11. Relax. If you've been in HR for any length of time, you likely have the knowledge but don't realize it!

12. Keep a positive and open mind about the test and *know* you will pass if you take the time to read each question more than once, as well as the answers.

13. Take your flash cards with you so you can review them whenever you have free time.

14. After studying diligently, take some time off from work the week of the exam for final review, then take a break from study the day before the exam.

15. Set an exam time when you are physically and mentally sharpest during the day.

16. Eat a high-protein meal before your exam.

17. For SJIs, rely on best practice as defined in the SHRM BASK to identify the best action to take.

18. Read the question carefully. If a question asks for an action, choose a response option that is the best action to take. If a question asks for an approach or strategy, choose an approach or strategy accordingly as your answer.

19. Take an educated guess. Eliminate choices where you can.

20. Flag questions that you want to go back to before finishing each section.

21. Save enough time to answer flagged questions at the end of each section.

22. Remain calm and confident during the exam. Go with your gut.

23. Believe in yourself.

24. Relax. The test asks you questions so you can show (1) what you know, (2) what you know how to do, and (3) that you can perform competently using what you know and know how to do. The questions are *not* written to trick you.

25. Learn from this experience and celebrate no matter what happens!

Appendix 2

Fifty-Item Practice Test and Answers

Introduction

These practice item sets include a total of fifty test items that were previously administered on either the SHRM-CP or SHRM-SCP exams in recent years. Similar to the real exams, these twenty-five SHRM-CP and twenty-five SHRM-SCP practice items are divided into separate sections that are composed of either knowledge items (KIs) or situational judgment items (SJIs). The first section, at each exam level, contains a total of seven KIs and foundational knowledge items, the second section contains ten SJIs, and the third section contains another set of eight KIs and foundational knowledge items. By gaining exposure to SHRM-CP and SHRM-SCP test items, you can make an informed decision regarding the content that best reflects the work you currently perform in your role.

This practice item list is not reflective of the entire blueprint that is used to build the SHRM-CP and SHRM-SCP exams. In other words, these practice items are not a mini-exam, and they do not represent all knowledge or behavioral areas tested on the exams. However, the items will give you a flavor of how the questions are structured on the exam and allow you to practice your test-taking strategies as you answer them.

To get a better sense of the real exams, SHRM recommends that you take the practice items during a timed period. We suggest you allot one and a half minutes per question (seventy-five minutes total) to gauge your ability to answer questions under the time constraints of the real exams.

One very important caution: do not assume that the ability to answer this set of fifty practice items correctly equates to a passing score on the certification exam. Similarly, do not use the results to predict how well you will do on the certification exam itself. This list is composed of less than half of the number of items on the SHRM-CP and SHRM-SCP exams. Also, these practice items do not fully cover all of the competency clusters and knowledge domains that are represented on the real exams.

Additionally, the conditions in your at-home or in-office environment will not match or likely mirror the controlled environment in which a SHRM exam is administered. For these reasons, the practice items are intended to give a preview of the structure and format of test questions. It is not appropriate to use results to predict an outcome on your exam, and doing well on these practice items will not guarantee a passing result on your exam. Refer to Chapter 3 for more information on scoring and exam construction of the SHRM-CP and SHRM-SCP exams.

The answer key and rationales for the correct answers for knowledge and foundational knowledge items appear at the end of the fifty-item set. For situational judgment items, the answer key represents the best response or most effective course of action as determined by a panel of SHRM-certified experts.

For examinees who plan to test outside of the United States—you will see questions about US Employment Law and Regulations. Questions in this functional area do not appear on exams for examinees who reside outside of the United States. If you reside outside the United States and plan to take your exam outside of the United States, omit these questions and adjust your timing accordingly.

Good luck!

The SHRM-CP Twenty-Five Practice Item Set

Section 1: This section is composed of seven knowledge items (KIs).

1. A company wants to improve the quality of its candidate selection by implementing a pre-employment test. After receiving a list of tests approved by the legal department, which should the HR business partner do next to evaluate the suitability of the tests?

   A. Review validity evidence for each test.

   B. Discuss position requirements with the hiring manager.

   C. Analyze the tests for biased language.

   D. Pilot the tests with a sample of candidates.

2. An HR manager needs to address allegations of marginalization and unfair treatment of specific groups within the company. Which is the best approach that the HR manager should take to address the issue?

   A. Implement a comprehensive workforce program to encourage mutual respect in the workplace.

   B. Discuss the implications of the allegations on business with the senior management team.

   C. Facilitate focus groups with women to ensure that they feel they are being treated fairly.

   D. Assign more responsibilities to the marginalized group so they have more career advancement opportunities.

3. An employee requests to work remotely from another country to relocate with a spouse who recently received new employment there. Which action should an HR professional take to mitigate risk for the employer?

   A. Obtain certification to cover risks and liabilities.

   B. Identify a new payroll administrator in the region.

   C. Ensure compliance with the local payroll laws of the other country.

   D. Compensate the employee as an independent contractor.

4. Which term best describes how organizations effectively use social media to increase consumers' online conversations?

   A. Brand awareness

   B. Search engine optimization

   C. Intangible benefit

   D. Content marketing

5. An HR associate meets with an employee who expresses concern about the recent lack of flexibility in work schedules. Which job attitude is declining for this employee?

   A. Engagement

   B. Commitment

   C. Involvement

   D. Satisfaction

6. A company is in the process of executing a reduction in force (RIF). Which action should the CHRO take to mitigate allegations of discriminatory practice during the RIF process?

   A. Present a business case supporting the strategic necessity.

   B. Managers can decide which employees should be laid off based on their performance.

   C. Offer severance packages for all employees who voluntarily leave during the RIF.

   D. Ensure employees laid off sign an agreement not to file a discriminatory claim.

7. When an organization's HR staff members are unable to serve as investigators during a disciplinary investigation, which individual is most suitable to serve in their place?

   A. Manager of the individual submitting the claim

   B. Internal and external legal counsel

   C. Member of the company leadership team

   D. Loss prevention specialist

Section 2: This section is composed of ten situational judgment items (SJIs).

The following scenario accompanies the next two items.

The CEO of a small insurance company unexpectedly retires. There is no succession plan in place, but the company's CFO acts as the interim CEO while a search is conducted. The HR manager recommends the board of directors conduct an external search to hire the new CEO. The board of directors wants to offer the CEO position to a recent hire who has a business school degree but is relatively inexperienced in leadership positions. The HR manager offers to thoroughly evaluate several external candidates along with the recent hire and then provide the results to the board. The evaluation process will take about two weeks. The board agrees not to select a new CEO without first reviewing the HR manager's evaluations. The HR manager asks an HR analyst to help with the evaluation and recommendation process.

8. One week into the evaluation process, the CFO approaches the HR analyst and angrily demands to know why the CFO is not being evaluated for the CEO position. The CFO did not previously express interest in the position. Which action should the HR analyst take?

   A. Explain that the CFO should have expressed interest in the position earlier.

   B. Inform the CFO that HR will evaluate the CFO to the extent possible over the next week.

   C. Ask the board members whether they would consider selecting the CFO for the CEO position.

   D. Tell the board the CFO has expressed interest in the CEO position.

9. During the evaluation process, the HR manager asks each candidate to write a statement about their work values. There is no objective process for evaluating these statements. How should the HR analyst evaluate them?

   A. Ask each candidate to give a presentation on the statement and rate each presentation's quality.

   B. Assess each candidate's statement based on the HR analyst's judgment of the quality of writing.

   C. Rate each statement based on how it corresponds with the company's values.

   D. Task HR employees with rating each statement based on how well it fits with the company's mission.

The following scenario accompanies the next three items.

An HR recruiter has been with a company for four years. According to the HR manager's performance records, the recruiter's performance steadily increased for three years. In the fourth year, colleagues reported a significant decline in the HR recruiter's performance, observing less enthusiasm than typical for the recruiter and delays in responding to emails. The recruiter's supervisor informs the HR manager that the recruiter has been engaging less and does not seem to receive feedback. The HR manager decides to investigate and learn the root cause of the recruiter's behavior. The recruiter felt discouraged after not receiving a promotion in the previous performance appraisal cycle.

Despite this discovery, the hiring managers had nothing but great things to say about the recruiter's work ethic. After being with the company for four years, the recruiter hoped for a promotion. The recruiter tells the HR manager that the process was unfair and their supervisor could not justify the rationale for the ratings. The recruiter also informs the HR manager that their supervisor is not receptive to their ideas for more effective approaches to attracting talent.

10. The recruiter tells the HR manager that their supervisor is incompetent. How should the HR manager respond to the recruiter?

    A. Inform the recruiter that their comment does not positively reflect the company's culture.

    B. Ask the recruiter to schedule a meeting with their supervisor to resolve the situation.

    C. Inform the recruiter that their comment is inaccurate because their supervisor is an expert in the HR field.

    D. Mentor the recruiter on communicating with their supervisor to work better as a team.

11. After learning that the recruiter's performance issues are because the recruiter believes the performance evaluation process is unfair, which should the HR manager do to resolve the issue?

    A. Inform the recruiter's supervisor about the recruiter's opinions and advise the supervisor to meet with the recruiter.

    B. Send the recruiter resources for in-house skills training to help improve performance.

    C. Describe the rationale for the performance appraisal process to the recruiter.

    D. Provide the supervisor with training materials on the performance appraisal process.

12. Which is the most effective approach to ensure supervisors are actively implementing the practice of employee performance feedback through-out the evaluation period?

   A.   Institute a reporting system where employees can request supervi-sor feedback at any time.

   B.   Coach supervisors on improving their leadership skills to communi-cate feedback to their employees effectively.

   C.   Ensure supervisors meet with their employees before performance evaluation to discuss the process.

   D.   Establish quarterly performance reviews requiring supervisors to provide regular feedback to their employees.

The following scenario accompanies the next two items.

The leadership team of a large manufacturing company wants to improve its succession planning and develop its future leaders. The HR manager is leading the design and implementation of a voluntary mentoring program for its regional offices. The HR manager consults with department managers to assess their needs and develops a framework outlining the program curricu-lum and guidelines. For the initial phase, the HR manager suggests limiting the number of employees who can apply for the program and including minimum qualifications for both the mentee and mentor.

Mentees are required to have a maximum of five years of experience, and mentors must have experience leading project teams. The HR manager also proposes pairing mentors and mentees across functions and departments to maximize learning and promote diversity in thinking. The HR manager is going to conduct quarterly check-ins with each mentor and mentee pair to gauge progress and solicit feedback. The leadership team agrees to pilot the program for one year in the central office before implementing it in the regional offices.

13. Three months into the program, a mentee expresses frustration with the cross-functional mentor and requests a transfer to a mentor in the mentee's department. Which action should the HR manager take?

   A.   Facilitate a counseling session between the mentor and mentee to repair the relationship.

   B.   Meet with the current mentor to discuss whether the transfer request should be approved.

   C.   Recommend another mentor from a different department to adhere to the guidelines.

   D.   Tell the mentee to try to resolve the differences with the cross-functional mentor.

14. The HR manager has been tracking the progress of the mentor program throughout the year. The CEO would like the HR manager to give a summative report about the program to the leadership team. How should the HR manager convey the success of the program?

    A. Compare employee turnover before and after the program.

    B. Show how mentees increased their skill sets because of the cross-functional training.

    C. Display how mentors became more productive at work as a result of the program.

    D. Present data showing the increased work responsibilities undertaken by mentees.

The following scenario accompanies the next three items.

A large steel producer with multiple plants and sales offices is implementing a new order entry system. The CEO has decided to implement the new system in a two-phase approach at each plant location. The five employees at the first plant will learn the new system and train others. During phase one, the team receives training from the system's vendor and guidance from the plant's HR manager. After completing the training, the team will fully integrate the new system to enter customer orders. During phase two, the team trains other employees to operate the system. The plant has about one hundred employees who require the training. The CEO sets a deadline of two months for all employees to complete the training. The plant manager decides the old order entry system must be available until all employees complete the training on the new system. The CEO wants the HR manager to oversee the process and support the implementation of the new system.

15. One week into phase two, the HR manager discovers that all five employees continue to use the old system because they believe it is more efficient. Which action should the HR manager take?

    A. Reinforce to the employees they need to set an example for the company by embracing the new system.

    B. State that transitioning to the new system will be more difficult once the old system becomes obsolete.

    C. Ask the vendor to provide additional training on the efficiencies of the new system.

    D. Inform the employees that the CEO will not be happy with them if they do not switch to the new system.

16. During phase two, the plant manager tells the HR manager that there is an increasing delay in processing orders because of errors made by employees using the new system. The plant manager is frustrated by this issue. How should the HR manager respond?

   A. Explain that errors are unavoidable as part of the transition process.

   B. Create a new contract with the vendor for additional training on the new system.

   C. Offer to speak to the affected customers and explain the reason for the delay.

   D. Encourage the plant manager to coach the employees who made the errors.

17. The HR manager wants to provide training manuals to employees, but the vendor cannot provide translations of different languages. In the interim, which action should the HR manager take to best resolve the issue?

   A. Tell employees who are unable to read the manual to ask other employees for help.

   B. Host moderate-length workshops for employees who need assistance with understanding the manual.

   C. Find another vendor who is willing to provide translated versions of the training manual.

   D. Recommend that the company purchase translation software to support the different languages needed.

Section 3: This section is composed of eight knowledge items (KIs).

18. A company is preparing to expand corporate social responsibility (CSR) initiatives to include employee volunteer programs. Which should be the first step to engage employees in the new CSR initiative?

    A. Send an email detailing the CSR initiative and a list of nearby volunteer opportunities.

    B. Hold a mandatory meeting to identify employee commitment levels.

    C. Communicate with and involve employees early in the strategic planning.

    D. Customized a message that focuses on how employees personally benefit by volunteering.

19. A small organization is experiencing a high number of customer complaints and discovers that employees are not using the resolution options available to them. Which recommendation will most likely result in long-term improvements?

    A. Evaluate the employee training experience through stay interviews and a workplace culture survey.

    B. Encourage managers to give bonuses to employees demonstrating good customer service.

    C. Send an email to all employees reminding them of the company's mission to provide excellent customer service.

    D. Review job descriptions of customer service employees to ensure expectations are accurately explained.

20. Which should an HR manager consider when forecasting labor demand?

    A. Expansion of product range

    B. Compensation market trends

    C. Cost to acquire resources

    D. Remuneration and reward programs

21. Which is the primary reason that focus groups should be used instead of surveys when collecting employees' opinions, ideas, and beliefs on a new product?

    A. Focus groups make it easier to compare individuals' thoughts.

    B. Focus groups gather a broader range of feedback.

    C.   Conducting surveys is a lengthier process.

    D.   Conducting surveys is more susceptible to bias.

22. Which step should be included in developing a comprehensive emergency action plan specific to one local site?

    A.   Employee training

    B.   Workplace evaluation

    C.   Alarm system description

    D.   Evacuation procedures

23. Which benefit of inclusion and diversity training should an HR manager emphasize to convince the CEO that the training will improve organizational effectiveness?

    A.   Creates awareness and helps develop knowledge and skills to promote strategic advantage.

    B.   Informs employees of one another's cultural backgrounds and traditions.

    C.   Helps the organization maintain legal compliance and avoid costly fines.

    D.   Modifies employee behaviors when interacting with one another, leading to greater peer respect.

24. An HR professional is selecting an employee for a high-potential development program for a global corporation. Which primary skill should an employee have to participate in the program?

    A.   Interest in career progression and travel

    B.   Effective communication with employees from different cultural backgrounds

    C.   Strong adaptability and customer focus

    D.   Exceptional decision-making and organizational skills

25. Which source increases the chances of intergroup conflict?

    A.   Goal alignment

    B.   Sufficient resources

    C.   Perceived similarity

    D.   Task interdependence

The SHRM-CP Twenty-Five Practice Item Answers

Question Number	Item Data		Rationale
1	Domain	People	"Review validity evidence for each test" is correct because it informs the evaluator if the test is worth evaluating further. If a test is not valid, there is no need to assess other potential properties.
	Sub-competency	Talent Acquisition	
	Difficulty	Somewhat Hard	
	Key	A	
2	Domain	Leadership	"Implement a comprehensive workforce program to encourage mutual respect in the workplace" is correct because the program would take a multi-level approach to provide employees with awareness and behaviors that are conducive to sustaining an inclusive and diverse workforce at the individual, team, and organizational levels.
	Sub-competency	Inclusion & Diversity	
	Difficulty	Easy	
	Key	A	
3	Domain	Workplace	"Ensure compliance with the local payroll laws of the other country" is correct because the laws governing payroll in the host country may differ from those in the home country. Therefore, it is crucial to familiarize oneself with the payroll laws of the host country to avoid any legal issues.
	Sub-competency	Managing a Global Workforce	
	Difficulty	Somewhat Easy	
	Key	C	
4	Domain	Organization	"Brand awareness" is correct because organizations can quickly reach a larger audience "faster than the traditional methods." As a result, that audience will then spread the content, further spreading information about organizations to others in their network.
	Sub-competency	Technology Management	
	Difficulty	Somewhat Hard	
	Key	A	

Question Number	Item Data		Rationale
5	Domain	People	"Job satisfaction" is correct because it reflects the employee's emotions about the job characteristics, the flexibility of the work schedule being one.
	Sub-competency	Employee Engagement & Retention	
	Difficulty	Somewhat Easy	
	Key	D	
6	Domain	Workplace	"Ensure employees laid off sign an agreement not to file a discriminatory claim" is correct because, in accordance with US Employment Opportunity Commission guidelines states that as an employer, one can ask their employees not to file a complaint with the understanding of their (employer) responsibilities during the process.
	Sub-competency	U.S. Employment Law & Regulations	
	Difficulty	Hard	
	Key	D	
7	Domain	Organization	"Internal and external legal counsel" is correct because using internal and external legal counsel is important as they can provide objective analysis and address potential issues.
	Sub-competency	Employee & Labor Relations	
	Difficulty	Somewhat Hard	
	Key	B	
8	Domain	Interpersonal	
	Sub-competency	Relationship Management	
	Difficulty	Somewhat Hard	
	Key	D	
9	Domain	Business	
	Sub-competency	Analytical Aptitude	
	Difficulty	Easy	
	Key	C	

Question Number	Item Data		Rationale
10	Domain	Leadership	Situational judgment items (SJIs) require the examinee to think about what is occurring in the scenario and decide which response option identifies the most effective course of action. Other response options may be something you *could* do to respond in the situation, but SJIs require thinking and acting based on the best of the available options. Do not base your answer on your organization's approach to handling the situation but, rather, answer based on what you know *should* be done according to best practice. Panels of SHRM-certified subject matter experts rate the effectiveness of each response option, and the best answer is derived by statistical analysis of those expert opinions.
10	Sub-competency	Leadership & Navigation	
10	Difficulty	Somewhat Hard	
10	Key	D	
11	Domain	Interpersonal	
11	Sub-competency	Relationship Management	
11	Difficulty	Somewhat Hard	
11	Key	A	
12	Domain	Leadership	
12	Sub-competency	Leadership & Navigation	
12	Difficulty	Easy	
12	Key	C	
13	Domain	Interpersonal	
13	Sub-competency	Relationship Management	
13	Difficulty	Somewhat Easy	
13	Key	A	
14	Domain	Business	
14	Sub-competency	Analytical Aptitude	
14	Difficulty	Somewhat Hard	
14	Key	B	
15	Domain	Leadership	
15	Sub-competency	Leadership & Navigation	
15	Difficulty	Somewhat Easy	
15	Key	C	

Question Number	Item Data		Rationale
16	Domain	Interpersonal	
	Sub-competency	Communication	
	Difficulty	Easy	
	Key	D	
17	Domain	Leadership	
	Sub-competency	Inclusion & Diversity	
	Difficulty	Somewhat Hard	
	Key	B	
18	Domain	Workplace	"Communicate with and involve employees early in the strategy planning" is correct because it initiates an active two-way communication system and allows the company to gauge levels of commitment and craft suitable strategies to improve participation levels.
	Sub-competency	Corporate Social Responsibility	
	Difficulty	Easy	
	Key	C	
19	Domain	People	"Evaluate the employee training experience through stay interviews and a workplace culture survey" is correct because a positive experience increases employee engagement. It, in turn, leads to higher levels of discretionary effort by the employees, which is especially important in customer-facing environments.
	Sub-competency	Employee Engagement & Retention	
	Difficulty	Somewhat Easy	
	Key	A	
20	Domain	Organization	"Expansion of product range" is correct because it is related to the labor demand forecasting. When business owners are considering labor demand forecasting, things to consider are growth over a specific period, expanding services or products, and technology advancement to support the objectives.
	Sub-competency	Workforce Management	
	Difficulty	Hard	
	Key	A	

Question Number	Item Data		Rationale
21	Domain	Business	"Focus groups gather a broader range of feedback " is correct because it uses qualitative methodologies to gather opinions, ideas, and beliefs. Qualitative methods do not restrict the type of information that is collected and allow honest information to be shared.
	Sub-competency	Analytical Aptitude	
	Difficulty	Somewhat Easy	
	Key	B	
22	Domain	Workplace	"Workplace evaluation" is correct because it provides a comprehensive assessment of the workplace and describes how employees will respond to different types of emergencies.
	Sub-competency	Risk Management	
	Difficulty	Somewhat Hard	
	Key	B	
23	Domain	Interpersonal	"Effective communication with employees from different cultural backgrounds"is correct because the ability to communicate effectively and pay attention to both verbal and nonverbal cues can help break down any cultural barriers, regardless of differences in cultural background.
	Sub-competency	Global Mindset	
	Difficulty	Easy	
	Key	A	
24	Domain	People	"Candidates who can communicate with employees from different cultural backgrounds effectively" is correct because it is important for candidates who aspire to a leadership role to possess the ability to communicate effectively with employees from different cultural backgrounds. Lack of cultural sensitivity can be a deal-breaker. Even if a candidate has a strong desire for career growth and is adaptable and customer-focused, they may still be a poor choice if they have poor communication skills, especially with people from diverse cultures.
	Sub-competency	Learning & Development	
	Difficulty	Somewhat Hard	
	Key	B	

Question Number	Item Data		Rationale
25	Domain	Organization	"Task interdependence" is correct because when one group interacts with another group, there is a potential for intergroup conflict to occur.
	Sub-competency	Organizational Effectiveness & Development	
	Difficulty	Somewhat Easy	
	Key	D	

The SHRM-SCP Twenty-Five Practice Item Set

Section 1: This section is composed of seven knowledge items (KIs).

1. When revising an organization's benefits program to retain employees, which activity provides the most useful information?

   A. Developing an HR strategic plan

   B. Using benchmarking data

   C. Conducting internal focus groups

   D. Consulting with outside experts

2. A business unit in a company is seeking HR support. Which HR function provides the most effective partnership?

   A. Center of excellence

   B. Service center

   C. Field generalist

   D. Transactional

3. Which act requires employee permission to conduct a background check?

   A. Privacy Act

   B. Fair Credit Reporting Act

   C. Genetic Information Nondiscrimination Act

   D. Stored Communications Act

4. After meeting with two conflicting company senior leaders together and separately, the HR manager is now offering several options for consideration to resolve the conflict. What term describes the technique used by the HR manager?

   A. Accommodation

   B. Bargaining

   C. Arbitration

   D. Mediation

5. A company has several locations with specialized departments at each location and uses centralized decision-making. Which type of organizational structure is this company using?

A.   Functional

B.   Divisional

C.   Geographic

D.   Product

6. Which action should the recruiting team take to increase communications with job seekers?

A.   Respond to applicants in a timely manner during the selection process.

B.   Simplify the online application process by eliminating unnecessary data fields.

C.   Implement an updated applicant tracking system.

D.   Decrease the number of steps in the recruiting workflow process.

7. Which example best demonstrates a strategic approach to corporate social responsibility?

A.   A beverage company invests heavily in research and development of recyclable bottling materials.

B.   A school bag distributor gives away a free school bag for every piece that it sells.

C.   A car manufacturer grants a scholarship to graduating high school students.

D.   A group of leisure divers set out to do an underwater cleanup against marine debris.

Section 2: This section is composed of ten situational judgment items (SJIs).

The following scenario accompanies the next two items.

A company has experienced rapid growth over the past few years. As the company grew, the organizational structure became more hierarchical, with many levels of supervision. However, leadership worked hard to maintain an informal company culture supporting employees' freedom and flexibility. Although it is not outwardly encouraged, employees at all levels are free to engage in romantic relationships if those relationships do not interfere with their work. Given the company's rapid growth, the CEO and the HR manager have concerns that there is an increasing potential for power imbalances and conflicts of interest due to romantic relationships between subordinates and supervisors.

The company's code of conduct includes a harassment policy but does not have an explicit policy on romantic workplace relationships. The CEO calls a meeting with the leadership team and the HR manager to discuss whether to institute policies governing romantic relationships between supervisors and subordinates and gather suggestions on what those policies might look like.

8. Leadership is worried employees will not accept a policy that governs subordinate-supervisor romances since some supervisors are currently engaged in consensual relationships with subordinates. How should the HR manager respond?

   A. Inform the leadership team that the policy will be written with exceptions for current subordinate-supervisor relationships.

   B. Tell the leadership team that HR will explain the benefits of the policy to all employees before formally instituting the policy.

   C. Explain to the leadership team why employee buy-in should not take precedence over protecting the company's reputation.

   D. Indicate to the leadership team that HR will look for opportunities to reassign one party in each subordinate-supervisor relationship to avoid conflict.

9. During the meeting, some members of the leadership team expressed that the company does not need a policy governing romances between subordinates and supervisors. It is pointless because there have been no problems with such relationships in the past. How should the HR manager respond?

A. Describe to the leadership team how a subordinate may feel pressured into agreeing to a relationship out of fear of reprisal from the supervisor.

B. Notify the leadership team that a policy governing romantic relationships can be added to the existing harassment policy.

C. Tell the leadership team that subordinate-supervisor relationships can expose both parties to discrimination or sexual harassment claims.

D. Suggest the leadership team postpone the discussion until the next quarterly planning meeting to give leaders time to consider the information.

The following scenario accompanies the next three items.

A manufacturing company has concerns about the changes in their employees' attitudes, lack of job satisfaction, and the increase in turnover rate. To learn more, the company established a reporting channel where employees can anonymously submit their feedback. The executive leadership team reviews all reports. Shortly after the reporting channel went operational, one of the employees reported that the company was involved in unethical practices, specifically biased hiring and discriminatory promotion practices. In addition, the executive leadership team learned that a client had an unpleasant experience with one of their employees.

The client alleges that the employee made derogatory remarks regarding the client's background. The executive leadership team worries about these issues and becoming public knowledge. The executive leadership team instructs the HR manager to investigate. The executive leadership team also wants the HR manager to provide recommendations for improving the company's recruiting strategy and an action plan to streamline the promotion process.

10. A manager tells the HR manager that an employee's persistent insubordination is due to cultural differences. Which action should the HR manager take first?

A. Meet with the employee in private to discuss the insubordinate and rude behavior.

B. Facilitate a meeting with the manager and employee to discuss their concerns.

C. Advise the manager to communicate more authoritatively with the employee.

D. Ask the manager's other employees about their experiences with this manager.

11. The HR manager realizes that voluntary turnover is higher in some ethnic groups than others. Which approach should the HR manager take to develop an initiative on inclusion that also addresses this turnover finding?

    A. Encourage employees to refer applicants to underrepresented groups within the company.

    B. Advise managers to speak favorably about inclusion to employees.

    C. Provide a training program with strategies for engaging in inclusive behaviors.

    D. Review exit interview data to determine if there is evidence of discriminatory treatment.

12. How should the HR manager investigate the reports from the employee reporting channel?

    A. Analyze personnel records to determine the hiring and promotion rates for each group.

    B. Survey all employees in the company on demographic attributes.

    C. Review HR records for similar employee complaints from the past.

    D. Interview employees on their observations of the company's hiring practices.

The following scenario accompanies the next two items.

The administrative assistant for a small, family-owned company recently retired. The retired administrative assistant, along with several other employees, is a relative of the company's owners. The owners' son is currently being trained to lead the company after his parents retire. Rather than search for a replacement for the retired administrative assistant, the owners decide to hire their son's wife, who has no prior experience. Shortly after the new administrative assistant begins, the HR manager receives several employee complaints.

The complaints state that the new administrative assistant is dressing inappropriately and incorrectly filing or misplacing important documents. Some employees state they have even received complaints from customers about the administrative assistant's clothing choices. The company does not have an employee handbook or policy manual, so there is no dress code for the HR manager to enforce. The administrative assistant interacts with customers daily, so the HR manager must resolve the issue.

13. Which action should the HR manager take to address the administrative assistant's performance issues?

    A.   Inform the administrative assistant of their assignment to a performance improvement plan.

    B.   Request the administrative assistant to be extra careful when handling important documents.

    C.   Meet privately with the administrative assistant to ensure the administrative assistant is aware of the expectations and responsibilities of the position.

    D.   Discuss the complaints with the administrative assistant so that the administrative assistant is aware of the problems.

14. The owners' son becomes aware of the complaints and demands the HR manager share the names of any family members who filed them. How should the HR manager respond?

    A.   Explain to the owners' son that the request could be perceived as inappropriate.

    B.   Advise the owners' son that it is inappropriate for HR to get involved in the family's problems.

    C.   Meet privately with the owners to explain the situation and ask them to intervene.

    D.   Ask the owners' son to explain why he wants to know who filed the complaints.

The following scenario accompanies the next three items.

After assessing the results from a companywide job evaluation and the company's recent decline in revenue, the company's senior leaders have opted to implement a one-year salary freeze on certain jobs. Senior leaders decided to wait two years before instituting the salary freeze to give employees time to prepare. While most departments have only one or two jobs that will be affected, one of the smaller departments of the company contains several highly specialized jobs with high salaries that will be subject to a salary freeze.

The HR manager is concerned that the news of the salary freeze will impact the department's productivity and may result in higher employee turnover. The HR manager is wary of executing the salary freeze and its potential impact on employee engagement, which may cause the employees to feel undervalued and underappreciated. Senior management has been trying to avoid the salary freeze, as the increasing employee turnover rate will significantly affect the company in keeping up with customer demands.

15. Soon after the announcement, the HR manager received feedback from a group of employees that many employees plan to submit their resignations. What should the HR manager do next?

    A. Administer a satisfaction survey to uncover the underlying cause of the desire to depart the company.

    B. Meet with HR professionals from the company's competitors to inquire about the challenges they have been facing.

    C. Advise senior management to postpone the salary freeze until HR conducts an environmental scan.

    D. Prepare a business analysis for senior management comparing the impact of the salary freeze to alternative options.

16. Due to the salary freeze, the HR manager is concerned about how to fill the two department vacancies affected by the salary freeze. Which action should the HR manager take next?

    A. Lower the starting salaries of all new hires and exempt them from the salary freeze.

    B. Inform the recruiters to let potential candidates know that there is a salary freeze.

    C. Advise senior management to authorize higher starting salaries for the two vacant positions.

    D. Inform senior management to realign duties with their current staff until a new hiring approach is implemented.

17. A year after the salary freeze announcement, there has been a steady decline in job satisfaction and overall company performance. The employee survey indicates that morale is low. Which is the best approach should the HR manager take to resolve the issue?

    A. Present a summary of the data to senior leaders to begin a discussion on the impact of the salary freeze.

    B. Ask managers to gather evidence that suggests the cost to productivity will outweigh the benefits gained through the salary freeze.

    C. Advise the senior management team to meet face-to-face with the department's employees to thank them for their hard work.

    D. Work with senior management to implement initiatives to increase employee engagement and enhance morale.

Section 3: This section is composed of eight knowledge items (KIs).

18. Senior leadership asks the HR director to interview two managers whose departments have the highest turnover to investigate declining employee morale. The HR director prefers to hold a focus group with all managers. Which rationale should the HR director provide to support using a focus group?

    A. The two managers may provide conflicting information during their interviews, which would prevent the cause from being identified.

    B. The two managers may refuse to participate in the interview to protect themselves from criticism.

    C. The input from the two managers would provide two opinions but not a comprehensive view of the situation.

    D. The interviews would be inefficient because they would require a significant time commitment from the two managers and the HR director.

19. Which type of monitoring is most important for meeting an organizational change management project's primary objectives?

    A. Environment

    B. Budget

    C. Quality

    D. Schedule

20. An HR director notices that the performance of an HR manager declined after taking on a new job scope. The manager mentions a decline in motivation as the reason. Which is the first step the HR director should take to address the decline in motivation?

    A. Create a performance improvement plan for the HR manager.

    B. Increase the HR manager's total rewards package.

    C. Assign a new job scope to the HR manager.

    D. Assess the HR manager's competence to perform the new work.

21. Which team characteristic best supports creativity and problem-solving in global virtual teams?

    A. Contextual diversity

    B. Task performance

    C. Personal diversity

    D. Team climate

22. How does establishing team norms support the effectiveness of a group?

    A.   It sets the general policies and guidelines for the project.

    B.   It establishes acceptable behavior of the members.

    C.   It outlines the scope of the project.

    D.   It determines which team members perform which tasks.

23. Which is a similarity between job enrichment and job enlargement?

    A.   Both design the position to challenge employees in flat organizations.

    B.   Both rotate employees to different duties throughout the company.

    C.   Both provide employees with the opportunity for advancement.

    D.   Both are traditional methods for career progression.

24. What is the key component in implementing an effective crisis management plan?

    A.   History of previous natural disaster plans

    B.   Comprehensive list of crises the plan covers

    C.   Accurate employee personnel files

    D.   Concise, relevant documentation

25. Two major corporations are merging, and the CEO wants feedback from the HR director on managing payroll for the newly merged company. What action should the HR director recommend?

    A.   Conduct a workforce analysis to determine how many additional payroll staff to hire.

    B.   Suggest payroll services be added to the self-service portal for managers to process payroll individually.

    C.   Determine if outsourcing payroll transactions after the merger provides the most cost-effective solution.

    D.   Move payroll to the shared services department within the company.

The **SHRM-SCP** Twenty-Five
Practice Item Answers

Question Number	Item Data		Rationale
1	Domain	People	"Conducting internal focus groups" is correct because the individual needs of the employees provide direct feedback and consider the culture and work environment of the specific organization. The use of internal focus groups has overtaken benchmarking as a preferred method of data collection and input because it provides for the collection of feedback from the various subgroups of employees within the organization. It can enhance the organization's ability to recognize the diversity of its workforce.
	Sub-competency	Total Rewards	
	Difficulty	Easy	
	Key	C	
2	Domain	Organization	"Field generalist" is correct because they are field generalists who are specifically assigned to a business unit in the firm.
	Sub-competency	Structure of the HR Function	
	Difficulty	Somewhat Hard	
	Key	C	
3	Domain	Workplace	"Fair Credit Reporting Act" is correct because it requires employers to notify individuals and receive permission to conduct a background or credit check.
	Sub-competency	US Employment Law and Regulations	
	Difficulty	Somewhat Easy	
	Key	B	
4	Domain	Interpersonal	"Mediation" is correct because it is a key process in which a neutral party (the HR manager) works with the two opposing parties to resolve their conflict.
	Sub-competency	Relationship Management	
	Difficulty	Somewhat Easy	
	Key	D	

Question Number	Item Data		Rationale
5	Domain	Organization	"Functional" is correct because it supports organizations with a high level of centralization. Since the workers in the individual departments are more specialized, they are more likely not to understand the company as a whole, creating the need for centralized decision-making on behalf of the company.
	Sub-competency	Organizational Effectiveness & Development	
	Difficulty	Somewhat Hard	
	Key	A	
6	Domain	People	"Respond to applicants in a timely manner during the selection process" is correct because providing regular updates and feedback to candidates is vital to creating a positive candidate experience—candidates prefer receiving continuous updates and feedback on their status in the hiring process. It is also an opportunity for the candidates to assess if the employer is a good fit for them.
	Sub-competency	Talent Acquisition	
	Difficulty	Somewhat Easy	
	Key	A	
7	Domain	Workplace	"A beverage company invests heavily in research and development of recyclable bottling materials" is correct because strategic CSR allows the company to make the greatest social impact and reap the greatest business benefits. Investing in research and development to be able to use recyclable bottling materials meets both requirements.
	Sub-competency	Corporate Social Responsibility	
	Difficulty	Easy	
	Key	A	
8	Domain	Interpersonal	
	Sub-competency	Relationship Management	
	Difficulty	Somewhat Easy	
	Key	D	
9	Domain	Leadership	
	Sub-competency	Leadership & Navigation	
	Difficulty	Somewhat Easy	
	Key	C	

Question Number	Item Data		Rationale
10	Domain	Interpersonal	
	Sub-competency	Relationship Management	
	Difficulty	Somewhat Hard	
	Key	B	
11	Domain	Leadership	Situational judgment items (SJIs) require the examinee to think about what is occurring in the scenario and decide which response option identifies the most effective course of action. Other response options may be something you *could* do to respond in the situation, but SJIs require thinking and acting based on the best of the available options. Do not base your answer on your organization's approach to handling the situation but, rather, answer based on what you know *should* be done according to best practice. Panels of SHRM-certified subject matter experts rate the effectiveness of each response option, and the best answer is derived by statistical analysis of those expert opinions.
	Sub-competency	Inclusion & Diversity	
	Difficulty	Somewhat Hard	
	Key	C	
12	Domain	Business	
	Sub-competency	Analytical Aptitude	
	Difficulty	Somewhat Easy	
	Key	A	
13	Domain	Interpersonal	
	Sub-competency	Relationship Management	
	Difficulty	Easy	
	Key	C	
14	Domain	Leadership	
	Sub-competency	Ethical Practice	
	Difficulty	Somewhat Easy	
	Key	A	
15	Domain	Business	
	Sub-competency	Consultation	
	Difficulty	Somewhat Easy	
	Key	D	

Question Number	Item Data		Rationale
16	Domain	Leadership	
	Sub-competency	Ethical Practice	
	Difficulty	Easy	
	Key	D	
17	Domain	Business	
	Sub-competency	Analytical Aptitude	
	Difficulty	Somewhat Easy	
	Key	A	
18	Domain	Organization	"The input from the two managers would provide two opinions but not a comprehensive view of the situation" is correct because more input provides a comprehensive picture of the underlying issues. An opportunity to gain real-time feedback and explore ideas to solve problems, diverse thoughts, experiences, and knowledge can provide rich insight.
	Sub-competency	Workforce Management	
	Difficulty	Easy	
	Key	C	
19	Domain	People	"Environment" is correct because monitoring the external and internal environment would be most important in a change management project as changes in either represent the most significant potential risks to the project's success.
	Sub-competency	HR Strategy	
	Difficulty	Somewhat Hard	
	Key	A	
20	Domain	Leadership	"Assess the HR manager's competence to perform the new work" is correct because, based on the Expectancy Theory, the initial step towards motivating someone to complete a set of tasks is to ascertain whether the person possesses the necessary competencies and also believes in their own ability to complete the assigned tasks.
	Sub-competency	Leadership & Navigation	
	Difficulty	Somewhat Easy	
	Key	D	

Question Number	Item Data		Rationale
21	Domain	Workplace	"Contextual diversity" is correct because it refers to differences in the environments the team members live in, such as the different levels of economic development and other types of institutions and political systems of their countries. Thereby there is an understanding of a broader range of contexts and access to more diverse knowledge and experiences. As a result, contextual diversity allows for more views and perspectives, which aids creativity, decision-making, and problem-solving.
	Sub-competency	Managing a Global Workforce	
	Difficulty	Somewhat Hard	
	Key	A	
22	Domain	Organization	"It establishes acceptable behavior of the members" is correct because outlining acceptable behavior for team members helps to ensure individuals are identified with, and connected to, the larger group.
	Sub-competency	Organizational Effectiveness & Development	
	Difficulty	Somewhat Easy	
	Key	B	
23	Domain	People	"Both design the position to challenge employees in flat organizations" is correct because flat organizations often lack career advancement opportunities, so it's important to design challenging positions to keep employees engaged. Job rotation enriches a job but doesn't guarantee upward mobility. Non-traditional methods like job enlargement and job enrichment are used by companies with limited promotional opportunities to retain talented employees.
	Sub-competency	Employee Engagement & Retention	
	Difficulty	Hard	
	Key	A	
24	Domain	Workplace	"Concise, relevant documentation" is correct because elaborate crisis management documents are often labor intensive, not practical, and not value-generating activities.
	Sub-competency	Risk Management	
	Difficulty	Somewhat Hard	
	Key	D	

Question Number	Item Data		Rationale
25	**Domain**	**Business**	"Determine if outsourcing payroll transactions after the merger provides the most cost-effective solution" is correct because it is valid when considering the merger of two large workforces. This approach can save time and money, as outsourcing payroll services can be more efficient and cost-effective than handling them in-house. It also allows HR personnel to focus on more strategic tasks instead of spending time on routine payroll tasks.
	Sub-competency	**Consultation**	
	Difficulty	**Somewhat Hard**	
	Key	**C**	

Appendix 3

Glossary of Terms Used in the Exams

The following terms appear in the SHRM Body of Applied Skills and Knowledge (SHRM BASK), may appear on the SHRM-CP and SHRM-SCP certification exams, and are applicable to all examinees.

Term	Definition
ADA *(US examinees only)*	Americans with Disabilities Act
ADAAA *(US examinees only)*	Americans with Disabilities Act Amendment Act
ADDIE	Analysis, design, development, implementation, and evaluation model; a five-step instructional design framework that guides the design and development of learning programs.
ADEA *(US examinees only)*	Age Discrimination in Employment Act
ADR	Alternative dispute resolution; an umbrella term for the various approaches and techniques (other than litigation) that can be used to resolve a dispute, such as arbitration, conciliation, and mediation.
analytics	Tools that add context or subclassifying comparison groups to data so that the data can be used for decision support.
applicant	Person who applies for or formally expresses interest in a position.
arbitration	Method of alternative dispute resolution (ADR) by which disputing parties agree to be bound by the decision of one or more impartial persons to whom they submit their dispute for final determination.
assessment center	Process by which job candidates or employees are evaluated to determine suitability or readiness for employment, training, promotion, or an assignment.
ATS	Applicant tracking system; a software application that automates organizations' management of the recruiting process, such as accepting application materials and screening applicants.
balance sheet	Statement of an organization's financial position at a specific point in time, showing assets, liabilities, and shareholder equity.

Term	Definition
balanced scorecard	Performance management tool that depicts an organization's overall performance as measured against goals, lagging indicators, and leading indicators.
benchmarking	Process by which an organization identifies performance gaps and sets goals for performance improvement by comparing its data, performance levels, and processes against those of other organizations.
benefits	Mandatory or voluntary payments or services provided to employees, which typically cover retirement, health care, sick pay and disability, life insurance, and paid time off (PTO).
BFOQ *(US examinees only)*	Bona fide occupational qualification; a factor (such as gender, religion, or age) that is reasonably necessary, in the normal operations of an organization, to carry out a particular job function.
bias	A partiality, inclination, or predisposition for or against something.
business case	Tool or document that defines a specific problem, proposes a solution, and provides justifications for the proposal in terms of time, cost efficiency, and probability of success.
business intelligence	Raw data (which may be internal or external to an organization) that is translated into meaningful information for decision-makers to use in taking strategic action.
business unit	Element or segment of an organization that represents a specific business function, such as accounting, marketing, or production; also may be called department, division, group, cost center, or functional area.
buy-in	Process by which a person or group provides a sustained commitment in support of a decision, approach, solution, or course of action.
candidate experience	Perception of a job seeker about an employer based on interaction during the complete recruitment process.
career development	Progression through a series of employment stages characterized by relatively unique issues, themes, and tasks.
career mapping	Process by which organizations use visual tools or guides to depict prototypical or exemplary career possibilities and paths in terms of sequential positions, roles, and stages.
career pathing	Process by which employers provide employees with a clear outline for moving from a current to a desired position.
cash flow statement	Statement of an organization's ability to meet its current and short-term obligations by showing incoming and outgoing cash and cash reserves in operations, investments, and financing.
center of excellence	Team or structure that provides expertise, best practices, support, and knowledge transfer in a focused area.
CEO	Chief executive officer
CFO	Chief financial officer

Term	Definition
change initiative	Transition in an organization's technology, culture, or behavior of its employees and managers.
change management	Principles and practices for managing a change initiative so it is more likely to be accepted and provided with the resources (such as financial, human, physical, etc.) necessary to reshape the organization and its people.
CHRO	Chief human resource officer
coaching	Focused, interactive communication and guidance intended to develop and enhance on-the-job performance, knowledge, or behavior.
COBRA *(US examinees only)*	Consolidated Omnibus Budget Reconciliation Act
code of conduct	Document that summarizes the standards of business conduct for an organization, such as rules, values, ethical principles, and vision.
comparable worth	Concept that jobs that are primarily filled by women and require skills, effort, responsibility, and working conditions comparable to similar jobs primarily filled by men should have the same classifications and salaries.
competencies	Clusters of highly interrelated attributes, including knowledge, skills, abilities, and other characteristics (KSAOs) that give rise to the behaviors needed to perform a given job effectively.
compliance	State of being in accordance with all national, federal, regional, and local laws, regulations and other government authorities and requirements applicable to the places in which an organization operates.
conciliation	Method of nonbinding alternative dispute resolution (ADR) by which a neutral third party tries to help disputing parties reach a mutually agreeable decision, such as mediation.
conflict of interest	Situation in which a person or organization may potentially benefit, either directly or indirectly, from undue influence due to involvement in outside activities, relationships, or investments that conflict with or have an impact on the employment relationship or its outcomes.
COO	Chief operating officer
cost-benefit analysis	Approach to determining the financial impact of an organization's activities and programs on profitability by comparing value created against the cost of creating that value.
critical path	Amount of time needed to complete all required elements or components of a task, which is determined by taking into account all project-task relationships.
CSR	Corporate social responsibility; an organization's commitment to operate ethically and contribute to economic development while improving the quality of life of the workforce and their families as well as of the local and global community.

Term	Definition
culture	Basic beliefs, attitudes, values, behaviors, and customs shared and followed by members of a group, which give rise to the group's sense of identity.
diversity	The differences between individuals on any attribute that may lead to the perception that another person is different from the self.
due diligence	Requirement to thoroughly investigate an action before it is taken through diligent research and evaluation.
EAP	Employee assistance program
EEOC *(US examinees only)*	Equal Employment Opportunity Commission
e-learning	Electronic media delivery of educational and training materials, processes, and programs.
emotional intelligence	Ability to be aware of, control, and express one's emotions, and to handle interpersonal relationships judiciously and empathetically.
employee engagement	Employees' emotional commitment to an organization, which is demonstrated by their willingness to put in discretionary effort to promote the organization's effective functioning.
employee experience	Sum of all touchpoints an employee has with an employer, including those related to an employee's role, workspace, manager, and well-being.
employee surveys	Instruments that collect and assess information on employees' attitudes and perceptions of the work environment or employment conditions, such as engagement or job satisfaction.
employees	Persons who exchange their work for wages or salary.
EPA *(US examinees only)*	Equal Pay Act
equality	Equal treatment of individuals and groups.
equity	A relative form of equality that takes into consideration the needs and characteristics of the individuals, the context of the situation, and circumstances that result in disparate outcomes.
ERISA *(US examinees only)*	Employee Retirement Income Security Act
ethics	Set of behavioral guidelines that an organization expects employees at all levels to follow to ensure appropriate moral and ethical business standards.
evidence-based	Approach to evaluation and decision-making that utilizes data and research findings to drive business outcomes.
EVP	Employee value proposition; employees' perceived value of the total rewards and tangible and intangible benefits they receive from the organization as part of employment, which drives unique and compelling organizational strategies for talent acquisition, retention, and engagement.

Term	Definition
exit interview	Meeting held with an employee who is about to leave an organization, typically to discuss the employee's reasons for leaving and the employee's experience of working for the organization.
FCRA *(US examinees only)*	Fair Credit Reporting Act
FLSA *(US examinees only)*	Fair Labor Standards Act
FMLA *(US examinees only)*	Family and Medical Leave Act
focus group	Small group of invited persons (typically six to twelve people) who actively participate in a structured discussion in which a facilitator elicits input on a specific product, process, policy, or program.
gap analysis	Method of assessing a current state to determine what is needed to move to a desired future state.
gig economy	Free market system in which temporary positions are common and organizations hire independent workers for short-term commitments instead of full-time employees.
GINA *(US examinees only)*	Genetic Information Nondiscrimination Act
globalization	Status of growing interconnectedness and interdependency among countries, people, markets, and organizations worldwide.
governance	System of rules and processes set up by an organization to ensure its compliance with local and international laws, accounting rules, ethical norms, internal codes of conduct, and other standards.
hazard	Potential harm that is often associated with a condition or activity that, if left uncontrolled, can result in injury or damage to persons or property.
HIPAA *(US examinees only)*	Health Insurance Portability and Accountability Act
HR	Human resources
HR service model	Approach to structuring and delivering an organization's HR services to support organizational success.
HRBP	HR business partner; an HR professional who advises an organization's leaders in developing and implementing a human capital strategy that closely aligns with the overall organizational mission, vision, and goals.
HRIS	Human resource information system used for gathering, storing, maintaining, retrieving, revising, and reporting relevant HR data.
HRM	Human resource management
inclusion	Extent to which each person in an organization is and feels welcomed, respected, supported, and valued as a team member.

Term	Definition
individual development plan	Document that guides employees toward their goals for professional development and growth.
information management	Use of technology to collect, process, and condense information for the purpose of managing the information efficiently as an organizational resource.
integrity	Adherence to a set of ethical standards that reflect strong moral principles, honesty, and consistency in behavior.
IT	Information technology
job analysis	Process of systematically studying a job to identify the activities, tasks, and responsibilities it includes, the personal qualifications necessary to perform it, and the conditions under which it is performed.
job description	Document that describes a job and its essential functions and requirements, such as knowledge, skills, abilities, tasks, reporting structure, and responsibilities.
job enlargement	Process of broadening a job's scope by adding different tasks to the job.
job enrichment	Process of increasing a job's depth by adding responsibilities to the job.
job evaluation	Process of determining a job's value and price to attract and retain employees by comparing the job against other jobs within the organization or against similar jobs in competing organizations.
KPI	Key performance indicator; a quantifiable measure of performance that gauges an organization's progress toward strategic objectives or other agreed-upon performance standards.
KSAOs	Knowledge, skills, abilities, and other characteristics.
labor union	Group of workers who formally organize and coordinate their activities to achieve common goals in their relationship with an employer or group of employers, such as a trade union.
lagging indicator	Type of metric describing an activity or change in performance that has already occurred.
leadership	Ability to influence, guide, inspire, or motivate a group or person to achieve their goals.
leadership development	Interventions designed to help an individual gain the knowledge, skills, abilities, and other characteristics (KSAOs) to engage with people and persuade them to work toward a vision or goal.
leading indicator	Type of metric describing an activity that can change future performance and predict success in the achievement of strategic goals.
liabilities	Organization's debts and other financial obligations.
LMRA *(US examinees only)*	Labor Management Relations Act

Term	Definition
M&A	Merger and acquisition; a process by which two separate organizations combine, either by joining together as relative equals (merger) or by one procuring the other (acquisition).
manager development	Interventions designed to help an individual gain the knowledge, skills, abilities, and other characteristics (KSAOs) required to manage people and resources to deliver a product or service.
measurement	Process of collecting, quantifying, and evaluating data.
mediation	Method of nonbinding alternative dispute resolution (ADR) by which a neutral third party tries to help disputing parties reach a mutually agreeable decision, such as conciliation.
mentoring	Relationship in which one person helps guide another's development.
mission statement	Concise outline of an organization's strategy that specifies the activities it intends to pursue and the course its management has charted for the future.
MNC	Multinational corporation
motivation	Factors that initiate, direct, and sustain human behavior over time.
negotiation	Process by which two or more parties work together to reach agreement on a matter.
NLRA *(US examinees only)*	National Labor Relations Act
offshoring	Method by which an organization relocates its processes or production to an international location through subsidiaries or third-party affiliates.
onboarding	Process of integrating a new employee with a company and its culture, as well as getting a new hire the tools and information needed to become a productive member of the team.
organizational effectiveness	Degree to which an organization is successful in executing its strategic objectives and mission.
organizational learning	Acquisition and transfer of knowledge within an organization through activities or processes that may occur at several organizational levels. Ability of an organization to learn from its mistakes and adjust its strategy accordingly.
organizational values	Beliefs and principles defined by an organization to direct and govern its employees' behavior.
orientation	Process by which new employees become familiar with the organization and with their specific department, co-workers, and job.
OSHA *(US examinees only)*	Occupational Safety and Health Act (law) Occupational Safety and Health Administration (agency)
outsourcing	Process by which an organization contracts with third-party vendors to provide selected services or activities instead of hiring new employees.

Term	Definition
performance appraisal	Process of measuring and evaluating an employee's adherence to performance standards and providing feedback to the employee.
performance management	Tools, activities, and processes that an organization uses to manage, maintain, and improve the job performance of employees.
performance measures	Data or calculations comparing current performance against key performance indicators (KPIs).
performance standards	Behaviors and results defined by an organization to communicate the expectations of management.
PESTLE	Political, economic, social, technological, legal, and environmental analysis; a method used to assess external factors and their influence on an organization.
position	Scope of work roles and responsibilities associated with one or more persons.
PTO	Paid time off
realistic job preview	Tool used in the staffing and selection process to provide an applicant with honest, complete information about the job and work environment.
recruitment	Process by which an organization seeks out candidates and encourages them to apply for job openings.
regulation	Rule or order issued by an administrative agency of government, which usually has the force of law.
reliability	Extent to which a measurement instrument provides consistent results.
remediation	Process by which an unacceptable action or behavior is corrected.
remote work	Work that is completed away from a company's office or other dedicated workspace (also known as telework).
remuneration	Total pay in the form of salary and wages received in exchange for employment, such as allowances, benefits, bonuses, cash incentives, and monetary value of noncash incentives.
remuneration surveys	Instruments that collect information on prevailing market compensation and benefits practices, such as base pay, pay ranges, starting wage rates, statutory and market cash payments, paid time off (PTO), and variable compensation.
repatriation	Process by which employees returning from international assignments reintegrate into their home country's culture, conditions, and employment.
restructuring	Act of reorganizing the legal, ownership, operational, or other structures of an organization.
retention	Ability of an organization to keep its employees.
risk	Uncertainty that has an effect on an objective, where the effect may include opportunities, losses, and threats.

Term	Definition
risk management	System for identifying, evaluating, and controlling actual and potential risks to an organization, which typically incorporates mitigation and response strategies, including the use of insurance.
ROI	Return on investment; data or calculation comparing an investment's monetary or intrinsic value against expended resources.
selection	Process of evaluating the most suitable candidates for a position.
sense of belonging	Extent to which individuals feel that they are a part of, included in, and connected with people at their organization.
shared services	Self-service or call center operations that promote HR expertise and deliver improved services across an organization.
Six Sigma and Lean Six Sigma	A set of techniques and tools for process improvement that aim to increase quality by decreasing defects in processes. Lean Six Sigma also aims at increasing speed by eliminating waste.
social media	Internet technology platforms and communities that people and organizations use to communicate and share information, opinions, and resources.
socialization	Process by which persons learn the knowledge, language, social skills, culture, and values of a group or organization.
sourcing	Process by which an organization generates a pool of qualified job applicants.
stakeholders	Persons affected by an organization's social, environmental, and economic impact, such as customers, employees, local communities, regulators, shareholders, and suppliers.
stay interviews	Structured conversations with employees for the purpose of determining which aspects of a job encourage employee retention or may be improved to encourage retention, such as culture, engagement, leadership, organization, and satisfaction.
strategic management	System of actions that leaders take to drive an organization toward its goals and objectives.
strategic planning	Process of setting goals and designing a path toward organizational success.
strategy	Plan of action for accomplishing an organization's overall and long-range goals.
succession planning	Process of implementing a talent management strategy to identify and foster the development of high-potential employees or other job candidates who, over time, may move into leadership positions of increased responsibility.
sustainability	Practice of purchasing and using resources wisely by balancing economic, social, and environmental concerns toward the goal of securing present and future generations' interests.
SWOT	Strengths, weaknesses, opportunities, and threats analysis; a method for assessing an organization's strategic capabilities through the environmental scanning process, which identifies and considers the internal and external factors that affect the achievement of organizational goals and objectives.

Term	Definition
systems thinking	Process for understanding how seemingly independent units within a larger entity interact with and influence one another.
talent management	System of integrated HR processes for attracting, developing, engaging, and retaining employees who have the knowledge, skills, abilities, and other characteristics (KSAOs) to meet current and future business needs.
totalization agreements	Bilateral agreements between countries that are created for the purpose of eliminating double taxation of employees on international assignments.
training	Process by which employees are provided with the knowledge, skills, abilities, and other characteristics (KSAOs) specific to a task or job.
transformational leadership	Leadership style that focuses on challenging and developing members of an organization to attain long-range results through continuous evolution, improvement, or change based on the leader's vision and strategy.
transparency	Extent to which an organization's agreements, dealings, information, practices, and transactions are open to disclosure and review by relevant persons.
turnover	Rate at which employees leave a workforce.
ULP *(US examinees only)*	Unfair labor practice; a violation of employee rights that is prohibited under US labor-relations statutes.
unfair labor practice	A violation of employee rights that is prohibited under global labor-relations statutes.
validity	Extent to which a measurement instrument measures what it is intended to measure.
value	Measure of usefulness, worth, or importance.
variance analysis	Statistical method for identifying the degree of difference between planned and actual performance or outcomes.
vision	Description of what an organization hopes to attain and accomplish in the future, which guides it toward that defined direction.
VP	Vice president
WARN Act *(US examinees only)*	Worker Adjustment and Retraining Notification Act
work–life integration	Approach to create harmony among all areas of life, such as work, home and family, community, personal well-being, and health.
workforce planning	Strategic process by which an organization analyzes its current workforce and determines the steps required for it to prepare for future needs.
workspace solution	Modification of a job, job site, or way of doing a job so an individual with a disability has equal access to opportunity in all aspects of work and is able to perform a job's essential functions.

Appendix 4

List of Acronyms

The following acronyms appear in the SHRM Body of Applied Skills and Knowledge (SHRM BASK), may appear on the SHRM-CP and SHRM-SCP certification exams, and are applicable to all examinees.

There are three categories of acronyms—(1) terms that are never spelled out and always appear as an acronym, are standard across HR practice, and are commonly understood by HR practitioners; (2) common acronyms used in HR practice that are spelled out the first time they appear in a test item and then used as an acronym in the item thereafter; and (3) terms that are likely to only be familiar to some HR professionals and therefore are always spelled out.

Category 1: Acronyms that are never spelled out: CEO, CFO, HR, HRIS, IT, and VP.

Category 2: Common terms. On the exam, each of these terms is spelled out the first time it is used in an exam item. Its acronym will be shown in parentheses if the term is used again in that item; if the term is used only once in that item, no acronym will be shown.

ADDIE	analysis, design, development, implementation, and evaluation
ADR	alternative dispute resolution
ATS	applicant tracking system
CHRO	chief human resource officer
COO	chief operating officer
CSR	corporate social responsibility
EAP	employee assistance program
EVP	employee value proposition
HRBP	HR business partner
HRM	human resource management
KPI	key performance indicator
KSAOs	knowledge, skills, abilities, and other characteristics

M&A	merger and acquisition
MNC	multinational corporation
PESTLE	political, economic, social, technological, legal, and environmental
PTO	paid time off
ROI	return on investment
SWOT	strengths, weaknesses, opportunities, and threats

Note: For situational judgment items, the term will be spelled out and the acronym placed in parentheses the first time it is used in the scenario associated with that item. Then it will appear only as an acronym in the rest of the scenario and in each of the associated questions and possible responses.

Category 3: If SHRM has not included a term you or your organization typically use as an acronym on one of these preceding two lists, the term will be spelled out whenever it is used on the exam. This includes, but is not limited to, *cost-benefit analysis, center of excellence, emotional intelligence, individual development plan, information management, learning management system, realistic job preview,* and *research and development.*

Additional US Employment Law Acronyms for US-Based Examinees

The following acronyms are US-specific laws, regulations, or terminology that should be familiar to all US-based examinees. These terms will only appear as acronyms on exams for US-based examinees and will not be spelled out anywhere on the exams. Examinees who are outside of the United States do not need to be familiar with these terms.

ADA	Americans with Disabilities Act
ADAAA	Americans with Disabilities Act Amendment Act
ADEA	Age Discrimination in Employment Act
BFOQ	Bona Fide Occupational Qualification
COBRA	Consolidated Omnibus Budget Reconciliation Act
EEOC	Equal Employment Opportunity Commission
EPA	Equal Pay Act
ERISA	Employee Retirement Income Security Act
FCRA	Fair Credit Reporting Act

FLSA   Fair Labor Standards Act

FMLA   Family and Medical Leave Act

GINA   Genetic Information Nondiscrimination Act

HIPAA   Health Insurance Portability and Accountability Act

LMRA   Labor Management Relations Act

NLRA   National Labor Relations Act

OSHA   Occupational Safety and Health Act (*law*) or Administration (*agency*)

ULP   unfair labor practice

WARN   Worker Adjustment and Retraining Notification

Appendix 5

Online Resources

These online resources may be helpful to you as you study for the SHRM certification exams.

About the SHRM Certification Exams

Eligibility Requirements for the SHRM-CP and SHRM-SCP Exams
https://www.shrm.org/credentials/certification/eligibility-criteria

Recertification
https://www.shrm.org/credentials/certification/recertification

Which Exam to Take and Sample SHRM-CP Questions
https://www.shrm.org/credentials/certification/which-shrm-certification

SHRM Membership and Communities
https://www.shrm.org/membership

Preparing and Studying

SHRM Body of Applied Skills and Knowledge (BASK)
https://www.shrm.org/credentials/certification/exam-preparation/
body-of-applied-skills-and-knowledge

SHRM Learning System
https://www.shrm.org/credentials/certification/exam-preparation/
shrm-learning-system

Honey and Mumford Learning Styles video link
https://www.youtube.com/watch?v=-92dlFiN_p8

VAK/VARK Model
https://vark-learn.com/introduction-to-vark/the-vark-modalities/

Mind Mapping
https://www.sheffield.ac.uk/academic-skills/study-skills-online/mind-mapping

Active Recall
https://www.brainscape.com/academy/active-recall-definition-studying/

The Leitner System
https://www.virtualsalt.com/learning-strategy-10-the-leitner-flash-card-system/

Feynman Technique
https://fs.blog/feynman-learning-technique

Chunking
https://www.verywellmind.com/chunking-how-can-this-technique-improve-your-memory-2794969

Managing Test Anxiety and Procrastination

These articles and presentations offer various viewpoints on why we procrastinate as well as tips for overcoming it.

Why We Choke Under Pressure—and How to Avoid It
https://www.ted.com/speakers/sian_leah_beilock

Why You Procrastinate (It Has Nothing to Do with Self-Control)
https://www.nytimes.com/2019/03/25/smarter-living/why-you-procrastinate-it-has-nothing-to-do-with-self-control.html

Procrastination
https://www.psychologytoday.com/us/basics/procrastination

5 Research-Based Strategies for Overcoming Procrastination
https://hbr.org/2017/10/5-research-based-strategies-for-overcoming-procrastination

Preparing for Test Day: All About Prometric Test Centers

What to Expect

https://www.prometric.com/test-takers/what-expect

Test Center Policies

https://www.prometric.com/covid-19-update/test-center-policies

Frequently Asked Questions (FAQs)

https://www.prometric.com/test-takers/frequently-asked-questions

Exam Tutorial

https://www.prometric.com/sites/default/files/SHRM-Tutorial/launch_
assessment_delivery.html

About SHRM Books

SHRM Books develops and publishes insights, ideas, strategies, and solutions on the topics that matter most to human resource professionals, people managers, and students.

The strength of our program lies in the expertise and thought leadership of our authors to educate, empower, elevate, and inspire readers around the world.

Each year SHRM Books publishes new titles covering contemporary human resource management issues, as well as general workplace topics. With more than one hundred titles available in print, digital, and audio formats, SHRM's books can be purchased through the SHRMStore at www.shrmstore.org and a variety of book retailers.

Learn more at SHRMBooks.org.

Index